# Apollo Root Cause Analysis©

## Also Known As

# RealityCharting®

*The World Standard for
Effective Problem Solving*

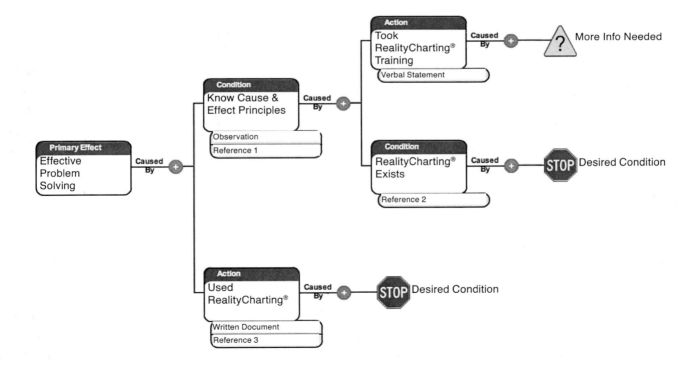

**Apollonian Publications, LLC
dba
RealityCharting®
www.realitycharting.com**

# Support and Contact Information

**For Additional Training, Software, or Consultation, Please Contact:**

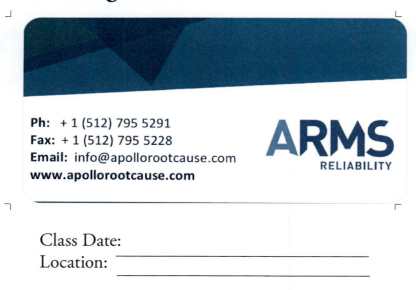

**Ph:** + 1 (512) 795 5291
**Fax:** + 1 (512) 795 5228
**Email:** info@apollorootcause.com
**www.apollorootcause.com**

ARMS
RELIABILITY

Class Date: _____

Location: _____

## For RealityCharting® Technical Support, Please Go To www.realitycharting.com/support

or contact us at:  www.realitycharting.com/contact-us
Apollonian Publications, LLC
8524 West Gage Blvd. A-289
Kennewick, WA 99336
1-877-722-2770

## Your RealityCharting® Software Information

Download RealityCharting® along with Adobe AIR from:
http://www.realitycharting.com/downloads/V7Download

Use this license to unlock and register your software:
**221S1P-P92492-16UPPX-10PVX0**

For Technical Support go to
http://www.realitycharting.com/support

Apollonian Publications, LLC

# Please Play Fair

The author has worked very hard to bring you this helpful information. Please respect his hard work as much as he respects yours. Please do not reproduce any of this material without permission from the publisher.

This Manual is an integral part of a training service and provides the required reference material and exercises for each student during and after the training. As such, it belongs to the student and may not be reused, resold or redistributed in any way. Any such use is a violation of the sale agreement. Students who do not leave class with this manual should notify Apollonian Publications, LLC at www.realitycharting.com.

To ensure consistency and quality of training, all ACRA™ Instructors are accredited by Dean L. Gano, with varying degrees of skill and knowledge. To learn more about your instructor's qualifications, go to www.realitycharting. com/accreditation/instructors

Following successful completion of this training class, you may want to establish yourself as an Accredited Investigator and Accredited Facilitator. Please talk to your instructor for further details, or go to www.realitycharting. com/training/accreditation for more details.

# Contents

Apollonian Publications, LLC

## Chapter 4 Step 2: Create a Realitychart     51

## Chapter 5 Step 3: Identify Effective Solutions     79

Apollonian Publications, LLC

# Preface

While formally investigating the Three Mile Island Nuclear Power Plant incident of 1979, Dean L. Gano, the creator of this methodology, was puzzled to find that all the root cause analysis methods in use at the time were people-centric methods that relied upon guessing and voting. Over the next decade of studying and teaching human problem solving, he uncovered the principles of causation rooted in human history, and created the Realitycharting process.

In every human endeavor, the ability to solve problems effectively is fundamental to our success. Unfortunately, we operate with the misguided belief that problem solving is a search for the "right" answer. In event-based problems we humans believe that a "Root Cause" provides a path to the correct answer.

As you learn more about the Realitycharting process, you will begin to realize the false hope of this categorical mindset. It is not the root cause we seek, it is effective solutions that prevent recurrence, are within our control, meet our goals and objectives, and do not cause other problems. Effective solutions are not necessarily at the end of a cause chain. They can be anywhere in the causal chain, and they must be legitimately connected by evidence-based causes and causal relationships. The Realitycharting method provides simple tools and the knowledge necessary to find effective solutions. It does this by creating a common reality that everyone can see so the best solutions are found and agreed to.

The success of the Realitycharting method has been proven throughout many industries over the past two decades, earning millions of dollars for those who have chosen to use it. The average earnings for each problem solved is US$35,000. One student put these methods to work on a 60 year old problem that everyone had given up on. Within a week, he had a creative solution that earned his company an additional US$1,000,000 per year.

The material presented herein is based on a proven understanding of the cause and effect principles rather than people-centric tools commonly called Root Cause Analysis. In this training course we learn there is no such thing as a single right answer. Rather, effective solutions are found in a structured set of known evidenced-based causes.

The methods, concepts and tools that make up RealityCharting have been developed by working closely with our clients from many different industries for over 20+ years. Because of our dedication to continuous improvement, our training methods have evolved beyond classroom training to include highly interactive, discovery-based, online learning.

When everyone in the organization understands the simple principles of causation and gains the skills to use the RealityCharting tools, a paradigm shift occurs that creates an effective problem-solving culture.

The goal of this training, and the tools that support it, namely RealityCharting®, RC Simplified™ and the RealityCharting Learning Center™ is to make you and your fellow workers the most successful problem solvers possible. Your success is our success.

By adopting the Realitycharting methodology, the culture evolves to understand that things do not just happen - rather an understanding that complicated issues can be easily understood and shared by creating a Realitychart. The end result is the elimination of repeat events and a steady structured path to continuous improvement. Ask your fellow workers to use RealityCharting Simplified™ [a free application] to replace the "Five Why's" or other simplistic methods. They can then send their reality of the problem and it's causes to you for further analysis using RealityCharting®. In the end, a new and simple way of thinking is developed that can truly change the culture.

Apollonian Publications, LLC

# Chapter 1
# Introduction

Ignorance is a most wonderful thing.
It facilitates magic.
It allows the masses to be led.
It provides answers when there are none.
It allows happiness in the presence of danger.

All this while the pursuit of knowledge can only destroy the illusion. Is it any wonder mankind chooses ignorance?
— *Dean Gano 1987*

# Chapter Objectives

- Understand the Course Objectives.
- Understand Problem Types.
- Understand the Causes of Ineffective Problem Solving.
- Understand the Illusion of Common Sense.
- Understand the Basis of Effective Problem Solving.

# Icons

Icons are used throughout this training manual to highlight key learning points. Watch for the icons defined below.

 Major point icon. Used to ensure you understand the main learning point(s).

 Caution Icon. A word of caution about how to use what you learned.

 Provocative Question Icon. Used to make you stop and think about a particular learning point. Also used to start a discussion and learn from the discussion.

 Think About This Icon. Unique examples used to support major points.

 Good Idea Icon. Used to highlight good ideas that can be utilized in the workplace.

 Remember This Icon. Used to reinforce the course learning objectives by summarizing what was just learned.

 Exercise Icon. Used to identify an exercise. Get ready to use your mind.

 RealityCharting® Icon. Used to identify key features of RealityCharting® that facilitate your problem solving efforts.

 Watch Help Video Icon. Used to identify when to watch a RealityCharting Help Video.

Apollonian Publications, LLC

# Introduction

Problem solving is generally understood to mean overcoming some kind of difficulty, but as you will see, it is really about controlling causes. The best solutions are often the unseen ones. We call these creative solutions because they are seemingly created from inside our minds. However, like the sculptor's notion that the statue lies within the stone, many effective solutions are waiting to be revealed within an infinite set of causes. To discover them requires the courage to leave old belief systems behind. Please join us on an adventure into a new way of thinking.

There are many kinds of problems and many ways to solve them. Most of the time our approach to problem solving is rule-based. Unfortunately, our world is event-based, and things seldom follow the rules. Some people believe this is caused by chance. We know better, and that is what this course is about.

We are going to look at event-based problems. These are the endless day-to-day problems that challenge our knowledge and skills. Event-based problems occur from an interaction of conditions and actions at a particular place and time frame. They are the broken piece of equipment, the broken leg, the computer problem, the procedural problem, or the personnel problem.

Event-based problems differ from rule-based problems. In rule-based problems we agree to a convention and thus a single solution is usually available. For example, in rule based problems, 2 + 2 = 4, or if we run a red light we may be fined, or if we violate a procedure something may go wrong. In each case, the answer is predefined by a set of rules.

In our day-to-day event-based world there are multiple correct answers to any defined problem. In the world of events, there are few rules, and the only rules we can be sure of are the cause and effect principles.

Causes and effects are the same thing, but seen from a different perspective. When we define a problem and begin looking for causes, we ask why the effect exists or occurred, and answer with a cause. Effects become causes as we continue to ask why, and a cause and effect chain is established. The point at which we start asking why is called the primary effect, and is determined by our perspective.

For example, if an injury is caused by a fall, and the fall is caused by a wet surface, and the wet surface is caused by a leaky valve, which is caused by inadequate maintenance activity, we may choose to improve our maintenance activities to prevent recurrence of the fall. In this event, we have identified a problem as an injury (the primary effect), some cause and effect relationships, and a solution that is attached to one of the causes (a root cause) that helps prevent the problem from recurring.

But, there is more to this simple relationship. Look closer and see how I chose to start with the injury as the primary effect. Now if I were the maintenance foreman, I may have started with the leaky valve and asked why did my maintenance activities fail. In doing so, I started at a different point in the cause and effect chain, but the problem is no less important than the injury. If I were the injured person, I may start by asking, "why does my ankle hurt." Regardless of where we start, events are an endless set of causes and where we start and finish is a function of our perspective.

# Introduction - Con't

Depending on our perspective we will define our own starting point and identify our own set of causes based on our experience.

While this example is useful in the beginning to understand the concept of cause and effect chains, it gets more complicated. The cause and effect principles dictates that for each effect in a cause and effect chain, there are at least two causes. These causes are either an action or a condition. For example, if we have a fire, there are three conditions and one action. The conditions are fuel, oxygen, and an ignition source. The action is what brings the three conditions together to cause the fire, such as a match strike or lightning.

Because there can be two or more answers to every "why" question, it soon becomes obvious that the chain is much more than a single series of causes. Indeed, the chain can grow exponentially resulting in an infinite set of causes.

At once we become overwhelmed with so many causes as to make this discovery seemingly useless. However, upon further inspection, we see that this infinite set of causes allows us to know why there can be many different solutions to any problem. We learn that no one has a monopoly on the right answer, and the "do it my way or the highway" philosophy can now be seen as a most foolish notion.

Since each cause in the cause and effect chain represents an opportunity for solutions, the door to innovation has been opened wide. And as we will learn, there are many ways to narrow this infinite set of causes to a manageable set. With this new understanding, we can focus on actions and conditions when asking "why," and by finding causes we can control, we prevent problems from occurring.

Indeed, controlling causes is what we humans do. It is the reason why we have become the most adaptive creature on earth. As an example, consider the baby spoon drop experiment. In the baby spoon drop experiment, a baby sitting in a high chair leans over with spoon in hand and drops it to the floor with great amazement.

While this may not seem like a big deal to the parents, it is a profound learning experience for the child. By repeating this experiment many times, the child learns to control causes. It learns that when an object at some height is no longer held in the hand, it will always fall to the floor. It also learns that in most cases a larger person (usually mom) will pick the object up and return it for further experimentation. While we do not understand the complete cause and effect chain at this time, we learn we can control objects and people. We learn we can cause things to happen by setting up conditions and actions. In doing so, what appears to be chaos becomes ordered by controlling the cause and effect relationships.

The more cause and effect relationships we understand, the better our chances of survival, and the more our responsibilities are clarified.

As John F. Kennedy said, "Things don't just happen, they are made to happen." Cause and effect relationships govern everything, and as such are the path to effective problem solving. This is what this course and the RealityCharting toolset are all about.

- Dean L. Gano

Apollonian Publications, LLC

# Objectives

## Course Objective

To provide the knowledge and skills necessary to find effective solutions to event-based problems every time.

## Learning Objectives

| | | Chapter |
|---|---|---|
| 1. | Know all the steps of effective problem solving. | 1 |
| 2. | Be able to clearly define a problem. | 2 |
| 3. | Understand the four principles of cause and effect. | 3 |
| 4. | Know the Realitycharting Process | 4 |
| 5. | Given a sample scenario, demonstrate competence in the creation of a Realitychart. | 4 |
| 6. | Be able to find effective solutions. | 5 |
| 7. | Know how to find creative solutions. | 5 |
| 8. | Know the key elements of an event report. | 6 |
| 9. | Know how to track solutions. | 6 |
| 10. | Know how to facilitate an incident investigation. | 7 |
| 11. | Know how to create an effective problem-solving culture. | 8 |
| 12. | Know how to use RealityCharting® software. | All |

# Common Problem Types

## Design Problems

- Use knowledge of the past to accomplish specific goals.
- Analysis often required.

## Creative Problems

- Use your imagination to create something new.
- Analysis occasionally required.

## Daily Problems

- These are simple events with simple solutions.
- Analysis occasionally required.
- What should I have for dinner?

## Rule-Based Problems

- Based on an accepted convention, such as math: 2 + 2 = 4.
- These normally have a right answer.
- Examples are violation of laws, procedures and rules.

**What about people problems?**

*People problems are found in just about every kind of problem but mostly in event-type problems.*

## Event-Based Problems*

- Problems of the past, such as an unacceptable event.
- These have no right answer - good, better, best.
- The purpose of event-type problem solving is to move from the current unacceptable state or condition to a desired condition or state.
- To ensure effective solutions analysis is required.

**\* Many events include all problem types.**

Apollonian Publications, LLC

# Example Report

## Typical Of Incident Reports Today

**Incident Date:** <u>10/28/11</u>  **Time:** <u>0817</u>  **Report Date:** <u>1/7/12</u>     **Facility:** <u>West</u>
**Team Members:** <u>LCT, JMG, DLG, JLG, JAS, MST, MAM</u>
**Description of Incident:**

On October 28, 2011, a contractor employee (FCT) was conducting an operational check on an elevator (ELH-23) at TCH-3-675 when a flashover occurred. The FCT electrician needed to check the door motor and switches on the top of the elevator car, requiring the elevator to remain energized in the performance of this difficult maintenance activity. While this was going on, a mail person from central mail (CMR-3), pushed the call button on the first floor ignoring the out of service sign posted over the call buttons. The FCT electrician heard a "buzzer" sound and was able to get clear of the moving parts on the top of the elevator car on which he was working before being injured, but, it was a close call. He was able to get control of the car from his location on top of the car, which allowed him to stop the car and exit safely. The main fuse blew, and the elevator shutdown.

Due to multiple parties involved in this incident, extensive discussions and management oversight has taken place. Since similar events have happened in the past we are confident we have a good(**3**) understanding of the problem(**2**).

**Type of Failure**(1):                **Predicted** ☐      **Failure** ☐
                    **Failure to Secondary Damage** ☐      **Other** ☑
**Description of Cause:**
A critique was held on November 30, 2011, at the location of the accident. The FCT electrician involved in the incident demonstrated step by step actions taken prior to the maintenance activity. The investigation discovered the problem to be human error(**1**), and corrective actions are being taken to preclude this from happening again.

**Corrective Actions:**
1. Provide refresher training to all employees on importance of warning signs.
2. Possible testing procedure to include a better lifted leads and jumpers control log.
3. Revise the electrical drawings to show the complete circuit for the elevator controls.
4. Position switches have been ordered to monitor the length of cable.
   With the completion of these changes, the problem will not reoccur.

**Root Cause**(1): Defective or Failed Part
**Approved:** Original Signed By BLB     **Date:** <u>1/7/12</u>

**Footnotes on Page 8**

# Causes of Ineffective Problem Solving

| Causes | Examples in Report |
|---|---|
| Incomplete Problem Definition | No "What" or "Significance" stated |
| Categorization – No Causal Analysis | See footnotes labeled "1" |
| Lack of a Questioning Attitude | Stopped too soon |
| A Need to Place or Deflect Blame | Problem defined as human error |
| Failure to Involve All Stakeholders | Written from a single perspective |
| Strong Bias to Past Experiences | Footnote 2; similar events repeated |
| Storytelling Culture | Description of Incident is a story |
| C & E Principle Not Understood | Causal relationships not stated |
| Dualistic Strategies | Footnote 3 "Good" understanding |
| Emotional Response | N/A |
| Belief in a Single Reality | N/A |

RealityCharting® helps you write a complete problem definition and helps prevent storytelling.

Is it right or wrong that the lion eats the gazelle?

The Realitycharting method addresses these and many other causes of ineffective problem solving.

Apollonian Publications, LLC

# Exercise 1.1
## Panatobe Plain

INSTRUCTIONS:
You live on the Panatobe Plain 5000 years ago and your objective is to obtain food. Which of the following things would you use to do so?

1. Knife
2. Map
3. Bow and Arrow
4. A 7 Year Old Boy
5. An 85 Year Old Chief
6. Shovel
7. Patience
8. Poison
9. Water
10. Animal Sounds

# The Illusion Of A Single Reality

### Belief In A Single Reality Causes Most Arguments

- Learn to appreciatively understand all perspectives.
- Use RealityCharting® to do this.

### A Single Reality Is An Illusion

- Effective problem solvers must recognize this illusion.
- We all view the world differently.
- Identical perspectives are not physiologically possible.

### Common Sense is an Illusion

- The notion of "Common Sense" is the product of known and repeatable cause and effect relationships.
- Sense is only "common" when we share an understanding of the effect of the same causal relationships.

 Conjoined twins don't hold the same view of the world, so why would we think other people with different life experiences, education, and emotional disposition could form some sort of common sense?

 Until we recognize that we all see problems from a different perspective and possess a different capacity to solve them, we will continue to realize less effective results.

Apollonian Publications, LLC

# Effective Event-based Problem Solving

## Appreciative Understanding

- Involve all stakeholders.
- Abandon the *Right-Answer* mind set.
- Embrace our ignorance.

## Know What We Are Solving

- Agree on the problem.
- Understand our goals.
- Align your goals with the problem.
- Write down the problem statement.

## Create A Common Reality

- Manage storytelling.
- Manage categorical thinking.
- Ask why until we reach our point of ignorance.
- Create a Realitychart.

## Solutions Based on Known Cause & Effect Relationships

- Align solutions with causes.
- Fix the cause not the blame.
- The Realitychart is the solution platform.

Embracing our ignorance means we value our lack of knowledge as an opportunity to learn rather than an embarrassment to be shunned.

# Effective Problem Solving

| Problem |
|---|

| Cause & Effect Relationships |
|---|

| Solutions |
|---|

**Why don't they teach this in school?**

*Because it is not yet common knowledge. Share what you learn in this class with others and direct them to the free stuff in the RealityCharting Learning Center™.*

 Apollonian Publications, LLC

# The Realitycharting Process

STEP 1. **Define the Problem**
Develop a common understanding of the problem and its significance

STEP 2. **Create a Realitychart**

a. Determine the causal relationships; Look for actions and conditions for each effect
b. Provide a graphical representation of the causal relationships
c. Support causes with evidence
d. Determine if causes are sufficient and necessary

STEP 3. **Identify Effective Solutions**

Challenge the causes and determine the "best" solution(s)

STEP 4. **Implement and Track Solutions**

Implement and track solutions for effectiveness.

Could it be any simpler?

# Exercise 1.2

INSTRUCTIONS:
Read this real report.

## Problem Statement From A Safety Report

"While placing material into a storage box, an employee inadvertently struck the storage box lid's locking mechanism, which caused the lid to close. The lid fell and struck the employee on the hand.

The employee received a hand laceration and was taken to an off-site medical facility for treatment. The injury was recordable, but did not result in lost time from work.

Routine work can present unexpected safety hazards, and employees must perform the required job tasks in a safe and controlled manner."

Apollonian Publications, LLC

## Analysis of Safety Report As Presented

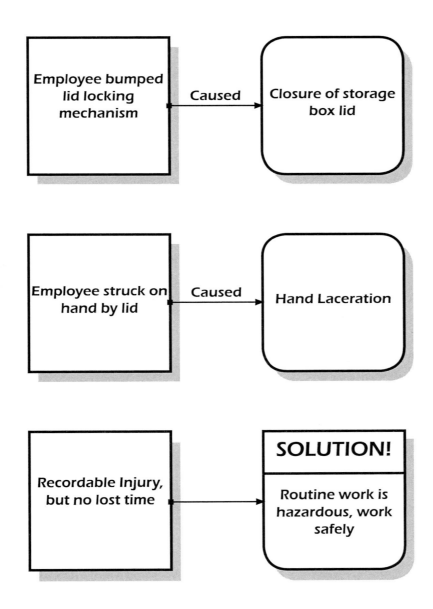

# Example
## Using the RealityCharting RCA Methodology

## Problem Definition

| | |
|---|---|
| **What** | Injured Hand |
| **When** | Normal Work Activity/ 07-10-11 @9:15 |
| **Where** | Planter Facility/ Area 10/ Instrument Room Tool Box |
| **Significance** | |
| Safety | Lost use of hand for 10 days, Recordable |
| Environment | N/A |
| Revenue | N/A |
| Cost | $2,500 US |
| Frequency | 1/ Last 5 Years |

## Realitychart

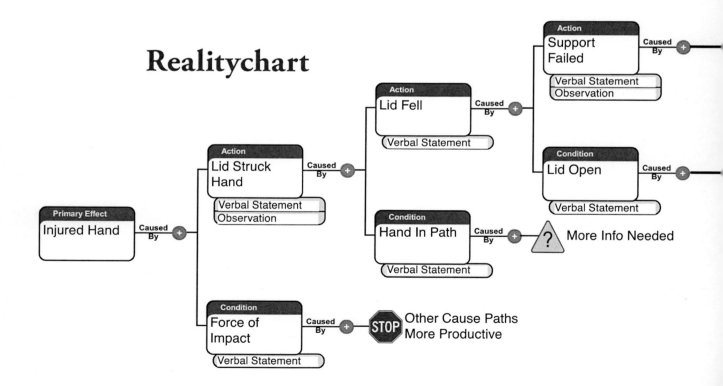

Apollonian Publications, LLC

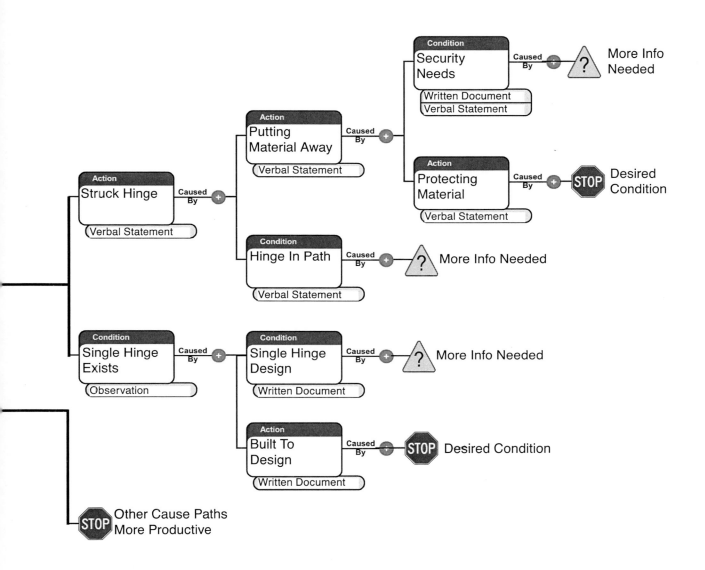

Remember, daily problems are always event-based problems. To become better at solving these problems we need to abandon the conventional wisdom of storytelling, categorization, placing blame, and the belief that everyone sees the world the same. By appreciatively understanding other perspectives, clearly defining the problem before asking why, and creating a Realitychart to document our common reality we can find effective solutions every time.

# Chapter 2
# Step 1: Define the Problem

"A problem well stated is a problem half-solved."
— *Charles F. Kettering*

## Chapter Objectives

- Understand the Four Elements of Problem Definition.
- Understand the Importance of Significance When Defining a Problem.
- Be Able to Clearly Define Any Problem.

# Exercise 2.1
## Problem Definition

### PART 1 INSTRUCTIONS

Read the following incident report and use it to fill in the Problem Definition fields in RealityCharting® or on the next page.

On Monday December 14, 2009 at 10 PM, 10 million gallons of raw sewage spilled into Seattle's waterfront after a switch at a treatment plant malfunctioned.

### PART 2 INSTRUCTIONS

When finished with part 1, read the revised incident report below. If you see a second problem here, create a new file in RealityCharting® to document a different problem. Use the Problem Definition fields or the blanks on the next page. To open a new file in RealityCharting® double click in the gray space at the top of the window.

Seattle - Tuesday, December 15, 2009
King County officials announced today that because of increased health risks, all public beaches at Alki Point, Fort Lawton, and Golden Gardens Park were closed indefinitely due to the release of about 10 million gallons of raw sewage into Seattle's waterfront. The release occurred Monday night at about 10:00 PM after a switch at a treatment plant malfunctioned.

### PART 3 INSTRUCTIONS

Let's do one more, only this time chose one individual from the following list, then read the report from this persons perspective and fill in the Problem Definition fields in RealityCharting® or on the next page.

Person 1: Sick Person in Hospital
Person 2: Maintenance Manager at the Sewage Treatment Plant
Person 3: Christmas Pageant Attendee
Person 4: King County General Hospital Emergency Room Nurse

King County General Hospital Emergency Room Nurses were overwhelmed Tuesday and Wednesday treating people with flu like symptoms. Most of the people interviewed lived on boats in the Shilshole Bay Marina which is located near the outflow of the Seattle Sewage treatment plant where on Monday, December 14, 2009, about 10 million gallons of raw sewage was released into Seattle's waterfront. Plant manager Sam Eglan says the spill lasted three hours, ending about 1:00 AM Tuesday after a switch at the treatment plant malfunctioned.
This was very disappointing news for people who live in the area because the annual Christmas pageant has been canceled for now. It is normally held at Fort Lawton beach on Wednesday night, but may be moved to a new location.
The Seattle Times reports the spill happened after a switch in a receiving tank malfunctioned, opening a gate that diverted all arriving untreated sewage directly into Puget Sound. Eglan says it took three hours to repair the switch.

Apollonian Publications, LLC

**What** _____

**When** _____

**Where** _____

**Significance** _____


**What** _____

**When** _____

**Where** _____

**Significance** _____


**What** _____

**When** _____

**Where** _____

**Significance** _____

# Defining The Problem

In typical problem analysis, we humans normally don't define the problem or do much analysis, rather we go right to the solutions.

Always write down the problem definition. The act of writing it down causes us to think at a different level because we know it will be scrutinized and since we don't like to be embarrassed, we do a better job of defining the problem.

Never ask who unless you are asking who knows the answer to a question.

## WHAT

- This is the Primary Effect - where we start asking "Why?"
- It is a noun-verb or verb-noun statement; e.g.: Car Wrecked or Wrecked Car.

## WHEN

- Time and Date
- Look for "Relative When's" because they help you formulate why questions. For example: "at night" might prompt you to ask if visibility was a problem.

## WHERE

- Specifically identify the location with proper nouns
- Look for "Relative Where's" because they help you formulate why questions. For example: "next to fire" might prompt you to ask if heat was a problem.

## SIGNIFICANCE

- This tells us why we are working on this problem
- Be specific and include costs and frequency.

Apollonian Publications, LLC

# The What

## The Primary Effect

- This is what we wish to not recur.
- It can also be something positive; i.e.: Met Goals
- There may be more than one for a given event.
- It is the point where we start asking "Why?"
- It may change as our analysis unfolds.
- It is a noun-verb or verb-noun statement; e.g.: Arm Fractured or Fractured Arm.

The *What* is the primary effect that we want to keep from recurring and the point at which we begin asking why.

## Primary Effect Examples

- Internet Server Failed
- Lost Production
- Shipment Delayed
- Lost Sales
- Exceeded Sales Goal
- Wrong Blood Type Administered
- Chlorine Gas Released
- Oil Spilled
- Corn Infested
- Production Goal Met

Can you think of more examples of a Primary Effect? List them below.

_____

_____

_____

# The When

## Chronological Timing

- We should always capture the date and time.
- We may need to be very precise.
- When did the what occur?

## Relative Timing

- What was happening when this event occurred?
  For Example: We may ask:
    - What were the weather conditions? e.g.: During a thunderstorm.
    - What was the system status? (Start-up, steady state, post maintenance, etc.)
    - Did the event occur after a holiday weekend?
- Knowing the When can help you formulate "Why" questions.
  For Example: Knowing the event happened at night might indicate a tired worker.

## When Examples:

CHRONOLOGICAL:
July 28, 2011 @ 4:32 PM

RELATIVE:
After a routine test run
During high wind gusts of 60 mph

Apollonian Publications, LLC

# The Where

## Specify The Event Location

- Document the specific location of the event.
  For example:
  - Facility
  - System
  - Component

## Relative "Where"

- "Where" may be expressed in relative terms. e.g.: Sitting next to a fire.
- Describe the conditions at the location. e.g.: In a smoky room.
- Knowing the Where can help you formulate "Why" questions.
  For Example: Knowing the event has happened at several locations might indicate a systemic problem.

## Where Examples:

ACTUAL LOCATION:
Facility: Southwest Warehouse
System: Utilities
Component: Panel 2

RELATIVE LOCATION:
Poorly Lit Area
By the Propane Tank

# The Significance

## Significance Answers The Following Questions:

- Why am I working on this problem?
- How much time should we spend on this problem?
- How many and what types of people should we use?
- How much money and effort should we spend?

## Be Specific

- Quantify costs, lost revenues and frequencies.
- Identify return on investment.

## Often Precedes The Primary Effect Causally

- If you ask why of the significance you often get the Primary Effect as your answer.
- Significance statements can be viewed as the consequences of the Primary Effect.
- You may need to restate your Primary Effect after writing the significance.

Apollonian Publications, LLC

## Generic Model

| | |
|---|---|
| Safety | No impact but serious potential |
| Environment | No Impact |
| Revenue | Lost Sales: US$30,000 |
| Cost | Materials: US$3,000; Labor: US$1,000 |
| Frequency | 2x in 2010, 3x in 2011 |

The category of Environment refers to the natural environment.

## Custom Examples:

### 1. Significance

| | |
|---|---|
| **Safety** | No Impact |
| **Customer Service** | No Impact |
| **Revenue** | US$90,000 Lost Revenue<br>(Reduced Rates 4 hours @ 30,000lbs/hr @ $.75/lb) |
| **Cost** | US$4,000<br>(Materials US$3,000; Labor US$1,000) |
| **Frequency** | 3x in 2010, 2x in 2011 |

### 2. Significance

| | |
|---|---|
| **Revenue** | US$575 Lost Profit; Order 36 hours late |
| **Cost** | Potential US$175,000/ year<br>(Client loss risk: 8% of Gross Business) |
| **Frequency** | 1x in 2010 (two near misses in 2011) |

RealityCharting® allows you to customize problem definition fields, like significance, to accommodate your business or organization.

### 3. Significance

| | |
|---|---|
| **Health** | Five workers infected |
| **Revenue** | US$12,500 Lost Profit<br>(250 additional hrs @ US$50/hr.) |
| **Liability** | Serious potential |
| **Frequency** | 1x in 1st Qtr., 1x in 2nd Qtr., 4x in 4th Qtr., all in 2011 |

## Use of Language - Be Specific

| No | Yes |
|---|---|
| ~~Injury~~ | Broken Hand |
| ~~Release~~ | 700 gallon Oil Spill |
| ~~Late delivery~~ | US$50,000 in Lost Sales |
| ~~Recurrent problem~~ | 7x in 8 months |

# Exercise 2.2
## Problem Definition

### INSTRUCTIONS

Read the problem description below and write the Problem Definition in the space below:

Two days ago, May 2, 2012 at about 8:30 am, Tyler was driving down North Avenue trying to identify street numbers when a car pulled into the road directly in front of him. Tyler swerved, missing the car, but drove directly into the edge of a concrete divider at the intersection of 25th St. and North Ave. Tyler suffered a broken arm but fortunately was wearing his seat belt and wasn't killed. He should be off work for about a week. This is our fifth recordable injury this year, but our first lost time event. Medical expenses are estimated at $12,000 US. Delivery vehicle #7 sustained damages estimated at approximately $3,500 US.

Tyler was driving our route 724 which has recently received complaints due to the last seven deliveries being late. This has occurred between April 17th and May 2nd this year. Tyler, one of our more punctual drivers, was moved to Route 724 in hopes of improving the delivery times. Three of the seven customers on the route have called recently to complain about the late deliveries. One of those, Mr. Jenkins, threatened to cancel his contract which is 10 % (US$250,000) of our delivery business.

I believe what happened was simply Tyler searching for an unfamiliar address while driving in light rain and heavy traffic. I have met with all the drivers and emphasized the need to be cautious under those kind of conditions. The regular driver for route 724, Gary Patterson, has received a letter of reprimand for the late deliveries in question.

| | |
|---|---|
| **What** | _____ |
| **When** | _____ |
| **Where** | _____ |
| **Significance** | |
| Safety | _____ |
| Environment | _____ |
| Revenue | _____ |
| Cost | _____ |
| Frequency | _____ |

Apollonian Publications, LLC

# Where To Start

## Guidelines

- There is no "right" place to start.
- Determine what you do not want to happen again and make it your primary effect.
- What would the boss tell you the problem is?
- Which "Proposed What" would fall furthest to the left on the chart?
- Start where you exceed a threshold criterion.

Don't worry about where you start. You can always come back and change it after you have a more developed Realitychart.

# Example Threshold Criteria

## RCA Trigger Process Example

What should happen to your threshold criteria if you continue to prevent problem recurrence?

You should establish a threshold value for each sub-category of significance as applicable to your goals and objectives.

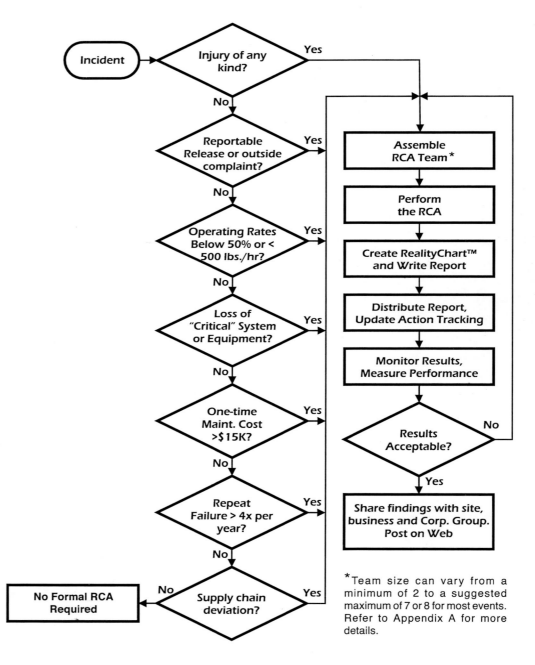

*Team size can vary from a minimum of 2 to a suggested maximum of 7 or 8 for most events. Refer to Appendix A for more details.

Apollonian Publications, LLC

# Example
## Problem Definitions

| | |
|---|---|
| **What** | Late Deliveries |
| **When** | Deliveries between 4/27 & 5/02/2012 |
| | While making daytime deliveries |
| **Where** | Route 724, Vehicle 7 |
| **Significance** | |
| Safety | No Impact |
| Environment | No Impact |
| Revenue | No Impact / Potential loss: US$250,000; approx. 10% of Total Revenue |
| Cost | No Impact |
| Frequency | 7 in 15 days |
| **What** | Broken Arm |
| **When** | May 2, 2011 @ 0830 AM |
| | While driving an unfamiliar route in light rain |
| **Where** | Rte. 724, 25th St. intersection of N. Ave. |
| **Significance** | |
| Safety | Lost time Injury; Broken left arm |
| Environment | No Impact |
| Revenue | No Impact |
| Cost | $12,000 US (medical expenses) |
| Frequency | 1st lost Time / 5th Recordable this year |

# Chapter 2: Define the Problem

 Watch the RealityCharting® Help Video titled Problem Definition.

 Remember to define the problem before you analyze it. Write down a *What, When, Where* and *Significance*. The *What* is where you begin asking *Why* and the *Significance* defines why you are working on the problem.

# Chapter 3
# The Cause & Effect Principles

"We cannot sow thistles and reap clover. Nature simply does not run things that way. She goes by cause and effect."
— *Napoleon Hill*

"All things are hidden, obscure, and debatable if the cause of the phenomena be unknown, but everything is clear if the cause be known."
— *Louis Pasteur's paper: The Germ Theory and Its Applications to Medicine and Surgery*

## Chapter Objectives

- Understand the Four Principles of Cause & Effect.
- Understand the Difference Between a Cause & Effect Chart and a Sequence of Events.

# Cause & Effect Principles

## Four Cause & Effect Principles

FIRST  Cause & effect are the same thing.

SECOND Each effect has at least two causes in the form of actions and conditions.

THIRD  Causes & effects are part of an infinite continuum of causes.

FOURTH An effect exists only if its causes exist in the same space and time frame.

 Apollonian Publications, LLC

# First Principle
## Causes & Effects Are The Same

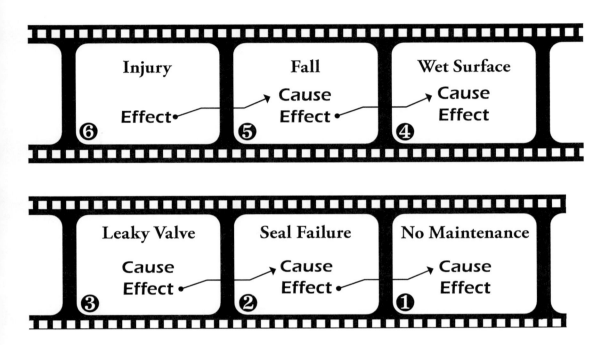

- An effect is the consequence of a cause.
- When we ask why of a cause it becomes an effect.
- Perspective determines the starting point.
- Sequence is from present to past.

**What does this principle teach us?**

*It teaches us that no matter where we start asking why, it is always in the middle of a chain of causes. Furthermore, the starting point is determined by the owner of the problem.*

# Second Principle
## Each Effect Has At Least Two Causes In The Form Of Actions And Conditions

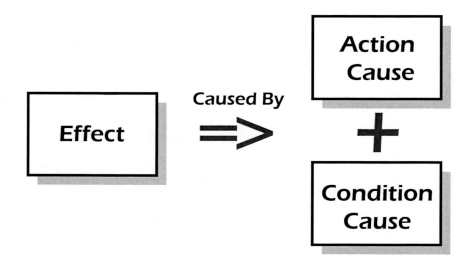

**What does this principle teach us?**

*This teaches us that every time we ask "why," we should find at least two causes in the form of actions and conditions.*

Apollonian Publications, LLC

# Example
## Actions & Conditions

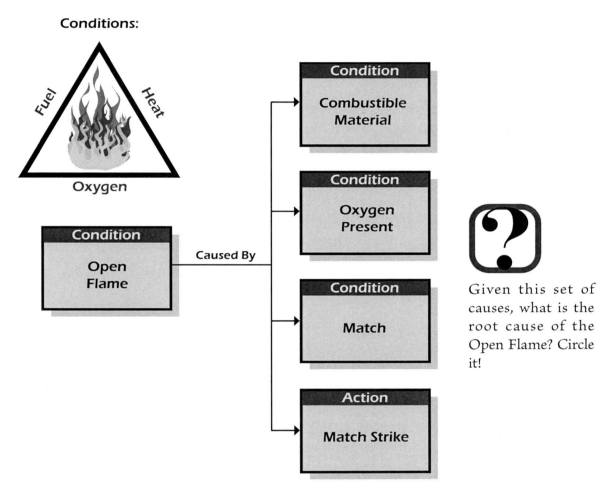

Given this set of causes, what is the root cause of the Open Flame? Circle it!

## Definitions

ACTIONS:

Causes that interact with conditions to cause an effect.

CONDITIONS:

Causes that exist in time prior to combining with an action cause to cause an effect.

# Exercise 3.1
## Action - Condition Exercise

**INSTRUCTIONS**
Read each causal set below and identify each cause as an action or condition by placing a check mark in the appropriate box.

| Causal Sets | Action | Condition |
|---|---|---|
| **Causal Set 1: Effect = Musical Note Played** | | |
| Key Pressed | | |
| Piano Exists | | |
| | | |
| **Causal Set 2: Effect = Lamp Turned On** | | |
| Lamp Present | | |
| Power to Lamp | | |
| Switch Turned | | |
| | | |
| **Causal Set 3: Effect = House** | | |
| Land | | |
| Concrete | | |
| House Constructed | | |
| Wood Exists | | |
| Nails | | |
| Manpower | | |
| Heavy Equipment | | |

Apollonian Publications, LLC

# Exercise 3.2
## Actions & Conditions

### INSTRUCTIONS

Fill in the action causes and condition causes for the primary effect in each of these examples. Only use 2 or 3 words in each box.

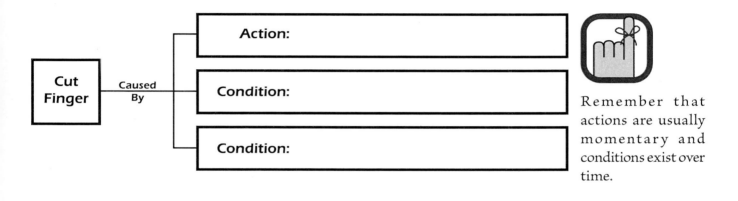

Remember that actions are usually momentary and conditions exist over time.

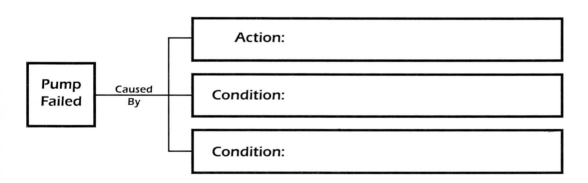

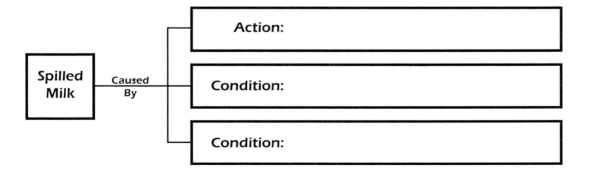

# Third Principle
## Causes and Effects are Part of An Infinite Continuum of Causes

### Causes are like pieces of a jigsaw puzzle:

- They connect in several ways.
- They are part of a bigger picture.
- The more connections, the better the picture.
- Individually they can be the beginning or the end.

 Event-based problem solving is like working a jigsaw puzzle. Connect all the easy or known causes, then focus on the hard questions.

 **What does this principle teach us?**

*It teaches us that in the beginning we may have many starting points, so don't waste time arguing over where to start – move on with finding causal relationships, then come back.*

 Apollonian Publications, LLC

# Infinite Set Of Causes

## Theoretical Example

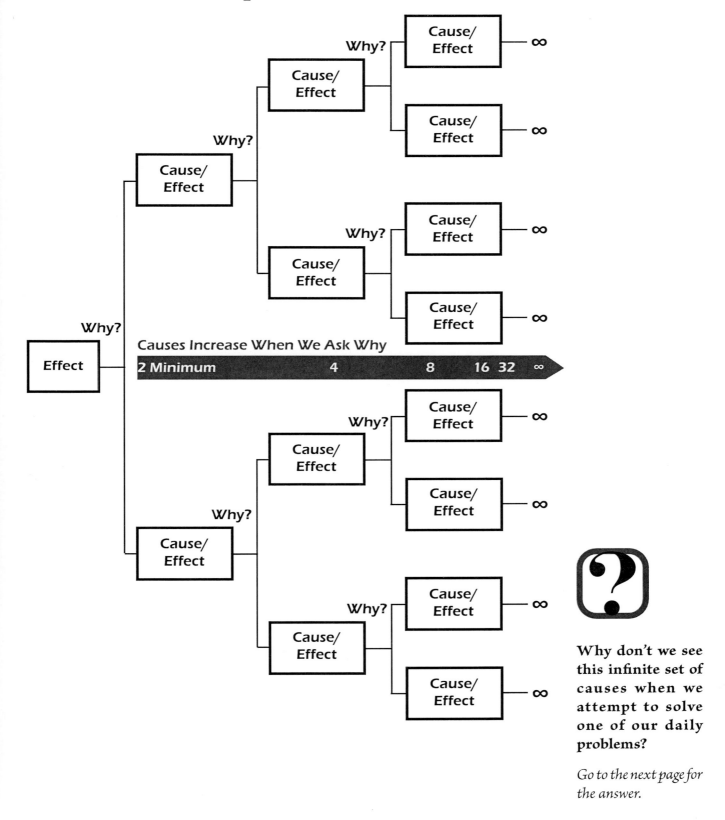

Why don't we see this infinite set of causes when we attempt to solve one of our daily problems?

*Go to the next page for the answer.*

# Filters
## Filters That Stifle A Questioning Attitude

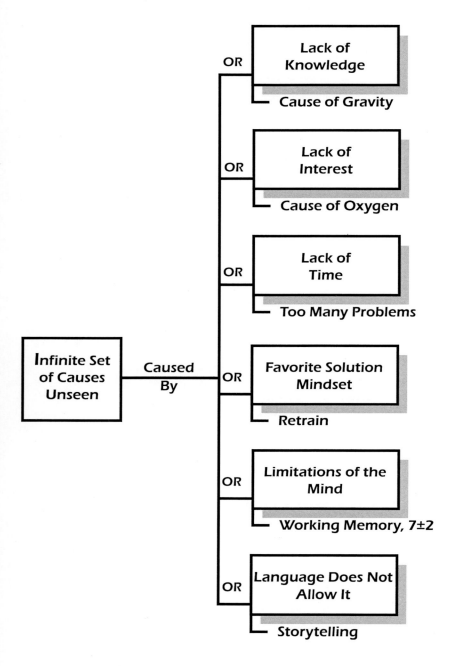

 From birth to about six years-old, the human brain is taking in information as fast as it can. The six year-old has more neural connections than at any other time in his or her life. At about age five or six the brain begins to spend more energy on sorting and categorizing incoming information than it does on retaining information. This is the beginning of discerning (filtering) and continues for the rest of our lives with the goal of trying to make sense of everything. Attempting to find meaning is a lifelong quest. The more successful among us adopt a causal strategy.

 Apollonian Publications, LLC

# Intermediate Causes
There Are Always Causes Between The Causes

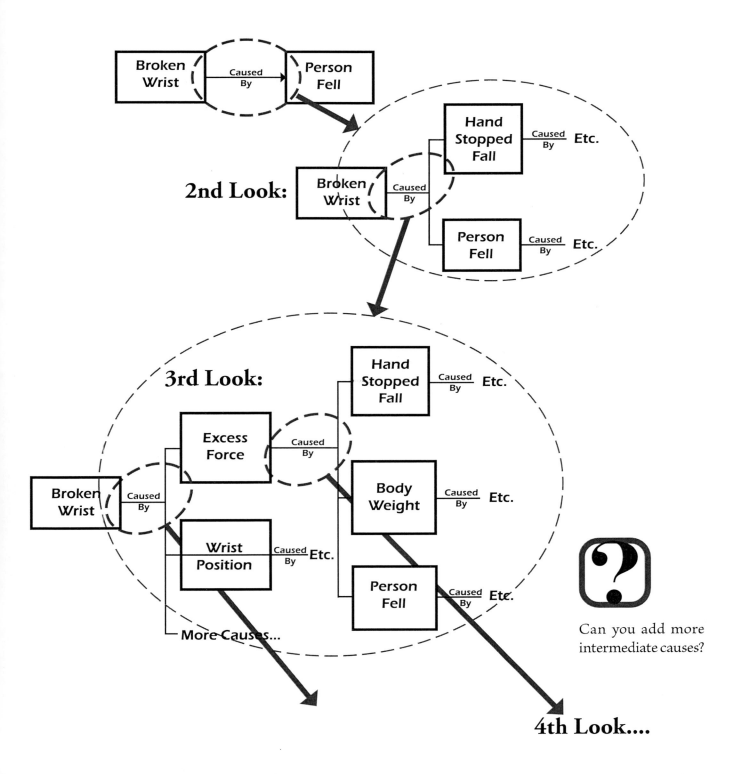

Can you add more
intermediate causes?

# Fourth Principle
## An Effect Exists Only If Its Causes Exist In The Same Space and Time Frame

How would you prevent the open fire?

_____

_____

_____

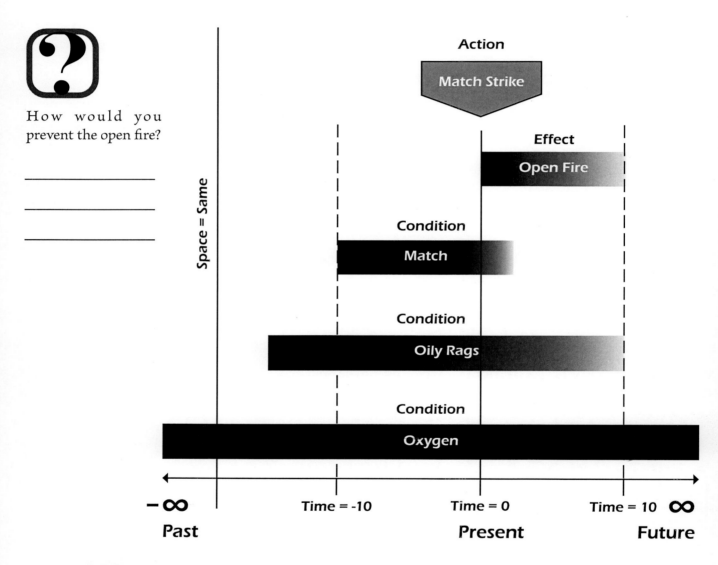

The causes of any effect must exist in the same place and time frame before the effect can exist. – Use this to check the validity of your Cause & Effect relationships. i.e.: If you remove a cause and the effect remains, it does not belong in the causal set. The Integrity Check feature in RealityCharting® helps you do this.

Watch the RealityCharting® Help Video titled Integrity Check.

Apollonian Publications, LLC

# Time Frames

The conditions must exist in the same time frame as the stated action cause

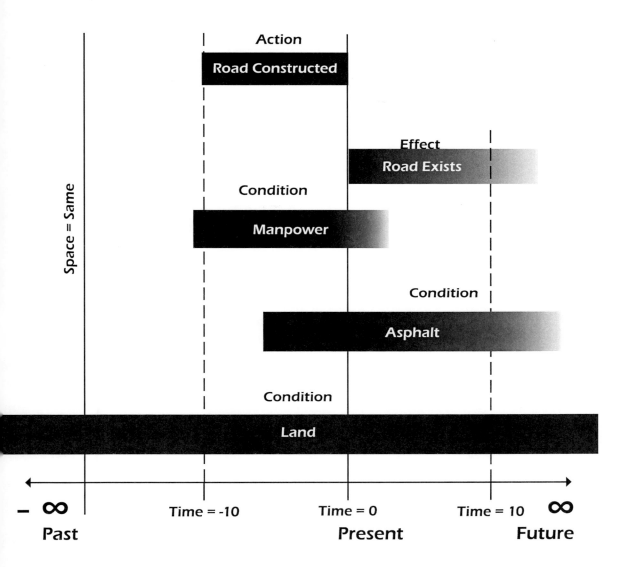

Action causes normally occur over a short period of time, but if we express an action that occurs over a long time frame, like this example, the conditional causes must correspond to the same time frame. That is, they must have the same when and where at the beginning of the event.

Apollonian Publications, LLC

# Exercise 3.3
## Ordering Cause & Effect Relationships

### INSTRUCTIONS

A Cause & Effect chart should be structured such that it flows from the present to the past. Arrange the causes below beginning with the most present cause in time. Connect causes with "Caused By" and make branches if appropriate.

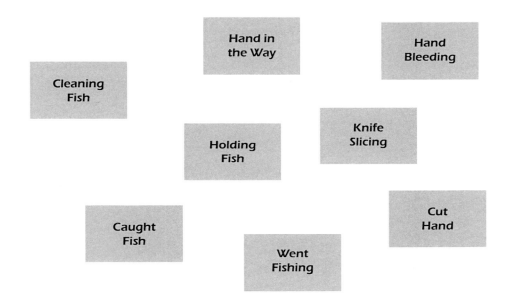

Time

**Present**                                              **Past**

# Exercise 3.4
## Time Line vs. Cause & Effect

### INSTRUCTIONS

Please read the sequence of events below which was taken from an actual industry report. Highlight the causes and arrange them in a cause and effect format on the opposite page. Start with the broken leg and ignore Dennis' injury.

| Date | Time | Event |
|------|------|-------|
| April 6 | 1800 hrs | Ben left pipe on the temporary scaffolding/cribbing, because he couldn't finish the job. (It was Sunday.) |
| April 7 | 0830 hrs | Fred decided we should finish Ben's work because he wouldn't be back for 3 days and it was in the way. |
| April 7 | 0850 hrs | Bob got on the Cherry picker (crane) to lift the pipe. |
| April 7 | 0852 hrs | I attached a sling to the pipe and gave Bob the OK to lift. I was using standard hand signals. |
| April 7 | 0855 hrs | The cribbing collapsed under the west end of the pipe. The west end of the pipe dropped and struck Tony in the legs. The other end of the pipe swung around and hit Dennis on the left knee. |
| April 7 | 0905 hrs | I called the Medical Technicians and they took Tony off to the Hospital. |
| April 7 | 1035 hrs | I heard from the hospital that Tony had broken his leg. |
| April 7 | 1100 hrs | Dennis reported he was a little sore, but otherwise okay. I met with the guys, and we agreed that since the injured men could not recall the sequence of events leading up to the accident, the exact cause could not be determined, but I am confident all safety procedures and policies were adhered to. |

A sequence of events is an excellent place to start because it provides many of the action causes. Use it to document the actions causes on your Realitychart and then look for the companion conditional causes.

Apollonian Publications, LLC

Remember, unlike a story or sequence of events, cause and effect relationships go from the present to the past and include both actions and conditions each time you ask why. First, identify what you know, so you can discover what else you need to know to understand the causes of the event. Knowing that an effect exists only if its causes exist in the same space and time frame helps ensure that we have the correct causes of an event.

While the notion of causation is generally understood to mean everything is caused to happen, by understanding the principles of causation we gain a much better understanding of our world and this understanding is the basis of a simple and effective problem-solving tool called RealityCharting®.

# Chapter 4
# Step 2: Create a Realitychart

"The world is as we see it."
— *Angelo Lucia*

---

## CHAPTER OBJECTIVES

- Understand the Realitycharting process.
- Understand the Role of Evidence.
- Demonstrate competence in creating a Realitychart.
- Learn How to Use RealityCharting®.

# Realitycharting
## Fundamental Components

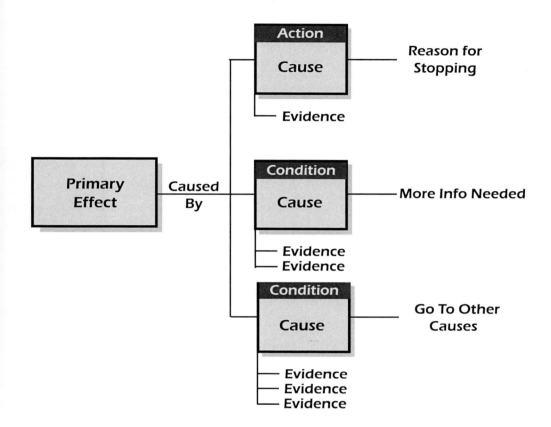

## Components Of A Realitychart:

- Primary Effect
- Action Causes and Conditional Causes
- Causal Connection - "Caused By"
- Evidence
- Cause Path Ending
  - Reason for Stopping
  - More Info Needed
  - Go To Other Causes on the chart

Always use RealityCharting® to create your chart because it will ensure you follow all the rules of construction.

Apollonian Publications, LLC

# Creating a Realitychart

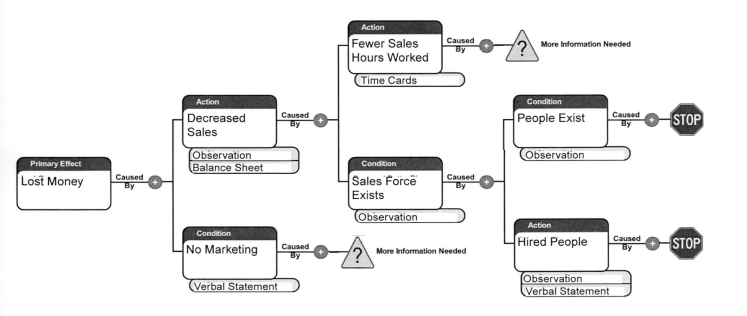

## Creating A Realitychart

- For each effect ask why.
- Look for causes in actions and conditions.
- Connect all causes with "Caused By."
- Support causes with evidence or use a "?" if unknown.
- End each cause path with More Info Needed, Go To, or a reason for stopping.

The Realitycharting process is an iterative one, so each step may be visited several times.

# Getting Started
## For Each Primary Effect Ask Why

### What is a Primary Effect?

- It is a singular effect of consequence that we wish to eliminate or mitigate.
- It is the problem name; The "What" in problem definition.
- It is the starting point from present to past in the chain of causes.
- It is the point at which we begin to ask "Why?"

### How Do We Choose the Primary Effect?

- There is no "right" place to start - it is your choice.
- It is where you choose to focus your why questions.
- The Primary Effect should reflect your goals and objectives.
- The perspective of all "Stakeholders" should be considered.
- The Primary Effect may be directed by others.
- Threshold criteria exceeded.

### Process Interactions

- Primary Effect can be changed at any time during the analysis.
- Often more than one Primary Effect in the beginning.
- Write them all down - Sort out later.
- Creating the Realitychart will determine if more than one problem exists.

RealityCharting® provides an easy way to synergize and capture causes in the early stages of an investigation.

Apollonian Publications, LLC

# Identify Causes
## Look For Causes In Actions And Conditions

## What Are Actions and Conditions?

- Both are causes; actions are often momentary & conditions often exist over time.
- Actions can become conditions if they act over a long period of time. Ex: Fire can be an initiator or a long term condition.
- Actions and conditions interact to create an effect.

Notice how this process is built upon the cause and effect principle.

## How Do We Find Actions and Conditions?

- Don't focus on finding actions and conditions - find causes first.
- Which ever one you find, look for the other in each causal element.
- Actions often end in –ed, such as "Hose Ruptured" or "Car Moved."
- Conditions are often the existence of the noun used in the action, such as "Hose Exists" or "Car Exists."
- Listen for causes in the story you hear from others.
- Develop a time line - each entry is usually an action.

RealityCharting® automatically provides for branched causes and uses a drop down menu to select action and condition causes.

## Process Interactions

- When you hear a cause, place it on the chart and immediately ask "why?"
- Ask "Why?" "Because?" and "Caused By?"
- During initial chart building accept all causes.
- Separate causes from the story by listening for a noun-verb statement

Do not get bogged down in searching for actions and conditions for each effect - they will come in time.

# Causal Language

### Noun - Verb Statements

RealityCharting® will limit the number of words you can enter in a cause box.

- Causes are expressed as Noun-Verb or Verb-Noun statements.
- Causal statements are typically 2 - 3 words.
- Avoid excess words to minimize the likelihood of multiple causes in a single cause box. Use abbreviations or acronyms for long names. e.g.: Polyvinyl Chloride - PVC.

### Conditions

- A conditional cause is normally a noun, or a noun phrase, with an unstated verb such as "exists" or "is."
- "Chemical Hose" is a noun phrase, the understood verb is "exists."

### Actions

Listen carefully for causes in the stories others tell. Because stories are more focused on setting the scene and giving you biased conclusions, they are often void of cause.

- An action cause must have a noun and a stated verb.
- "Hose Ruptured" is a typical noun-verb causal statement; a noun followed by an action.
- Action causes can be non-actions such as Step Not Performed

### Descriptive Language

- Adjectives and adverbs should be avoided.
  e.g.: "Specification Not Met" is better than "Poor Design." and is a non-action versus a category.
  - ◆ Note: "Sharp Knife" or "Worn Bearing" are examples of a noun phrase that include an adjective but are understood as a noun and therefore acceptable.
- Be very specific.

### Conjunctions

- Conjunctions such as And, Or, If, and Because can indicate a causal relationship - Do not use conjunctions.
- RealityCharting® will find these and many others and ask you to correct your statement.
- Conjunctions may indicate causes between causes.

 Apollonian Publications, LLC

# Define Causal Relationships
## Connect All Causes With "Caused By"

## Caused By

- "Caused By" forces your causes to go from present to past.
- "Caused By" elicits a more specific response.
- "Caused By" minimizes storytelling.
- "Caused By" is the glue for your Realitychart.

RealityCharting® automatically inserts "Caused By" between all causes.

## Constructing the Chart

- With knowledgeable team members use RealityCharting® and an overhead projector to gather and arrange causes.
- If you do not have the electronic tools write all causes on "Post It" Notes using a vertical surface so you can step back and see the big picture.
- Always use RealityCharting® to document, check validity, and share your understanding.
- Ask why until no more answers come, then,
- Starting at the Primary Effect, ask why again, looking for actions & conditions - We call this the square-one loop.
- Repeat until chart is complete.
- Add evidence anytime, but don't stop the flow of chart construction.
- If you don't have evidence, RealityCharting® inserts a "?" by default - This will generate an action item in RealityCharting's Action Item Report.

Use the Causal Elements View in RealityCharting® to ask why of each effect and verify the causes meet the rules of causation.

Watch the RealityCharting® Help Video titled Causal Elements View.

## Process Interactions

- Accept all causes from stakeholders; if they can be connected, they have value.
- Don't waste time trying to find every action and condition.
- The condition is often the noun used in the action statement. e.g.: An action of Chemical Spilled has a condition of Chemical Exists.
- Ask of a stated cause "And that was caused by?" to help participants focus better.

If you have an action cause and can't find a corresponding conditional cause, add the word exists to the noun in the action cause.

# Exercise 4.1
## Charting

### INSTRUCTIONS

Using the report below, define the problem and create a Realitychart using RealityCharting® if you can. After you have completed it, share it with your neighbor and compare.

## Event Report

On the morning of December 15, 2009, Sally Knox was driving her son to pre-school on Road 68. At milepost 37 the car lost power and she quickly drove to the shoulder of this narrow road. She put the car in Park and tried to restart it, but nothing happened. She pulled her cell phone out of her purse and called her husband at work to tell him what had happened. He said he had been working on the car the night before and asked her to get out of the car and look under the hood to see if she could see any loose ignition wires up by the firewall on the driver's side. She felt confident in his advise because he said he thought she could correct the problem very easily.

Just as she opened the door, a passing truck ripped the door off. The truck driver later said that he couldn't avoid hitting the door because it was in his path and he was moving too fast. She was not injured but was shaken to say the least. That night at home, after the police investigation and the tow truck took the wrecked car to the repair shop, her husband apologized for not securing the ignition wires properly while repairing the car. He said he was in a hurry because she was insisting that he come in the house to read the kids a story before they went to bed. Aside from the lost use of car and trauma to the wife, child, and husband, there were repair costs of $3,500.

Apollonian Publications, LLC

# Problem Definition

**What**
**When**
**Where**
**Significance**
    *Safety*
    *Environment*
    *Revenue*
    *Cost*
    *Frequency*

# Realitychart

The Problem Definition in RealityCharting® can be customized to add any data you may wish to capture.

# Exercise 4.2
## Charting

### INSTRUCTIONS

Using the report below, define the problem and create a Realitychart using RealityCharting® if you can. After you have completed it, share it with your neighbor and compare.

## Problem Report

On September 9, 2011, at the Moncrief site, a kitchen cabinet door hinge failed which caused the cabinet door to fall, striking an employee which resulted in a contusion and abrasion of the right shoulder. Fortunately the employee wasn't struck in the head. The employee was preparing lunch when this occurred.

The individual went to Health Services and received first aid. The effects were not serious but the employee was very disturbed by this unexpected event.

I conducted a site investigation and interviewed several employees and discovered this was a two-part door hinge designed for easy adjustment. This is accomplished by using a single set screw on the door plate which is then screwed into the cabinet mounting plate. The door had two hinges on it and is located above a counter and measures by ruler about six feet off the floor.

The room on the other side of the wall where these cabinets are mounted contains the heating and ventilating fans for Bldg. 11. These are large units and set up quite a vibration in the surrounding walls and floor.

I believe the hinge failed because the set screws were missing. They were found inside the cabinet on the lower shelves. By the looks of the threads I believe one of them was never installed.

## Root Cause

Hinge Failed

## Preventative and Corrective Action

1) Replace the set screws.
2) Inspect similar installations for prevention.

## Costs:

$200 US Medical Expenses

# Problem Definition

**What**
**When**
**Where**
**Significance**
> Safety
> Environment
> Revenue
> Cost
> Frequency

# Realitychart

# Provide Evidence
## Support All Causes With Evidence

### What Is Evidence?

- Evidence is any information that supports a conclusion.

### How Is It Presented?

- Sensed: It is processed through our senses of sight, sound, smell, taste and touch. Sensed is the highest quality evidence.
- Inferred: Our ability to infer is derived from our understanding of known and repeatable causal relationships. Inference is the next highest quality evidence.
- Intuitive: Intuition is also inference but it combines reasoning and feelings at the sub-conscious level. Intuition is typically unreliable and should not be utilized as evidence unless it is all you have.
- Emotional: Feelings and emotions are never effective evidence but should not be ignored. It is not uncommon for feelings to provide insight to viable cause paths. Use it to find more solid evidence.

### Why Is Evidence Important?

- Because it supports the reality of the cause.
- Because evidence-based causes ensure effective solutions so long as solutions are only assigned to evidenced-based cause paths.
- Because it helps expose politics and power plays.

 Always ask for evidence of a cause regardless of who provides it. If it is an expert opinion, ask to be educated.

Apollonian Publications, LLC

# Realitychart Evidence

## Applying Evidence To The Chart

- Evidence is attached to the bottom of each cause on the chart
- The same evidence may be used on more than one cause
- RealityCharting® provides an Advanced Evidence feature that allows you to choose from an editable drop down list of evidence statements

## Difficulties Recognizing Evidence

- Evidence and causes may be interchangeable

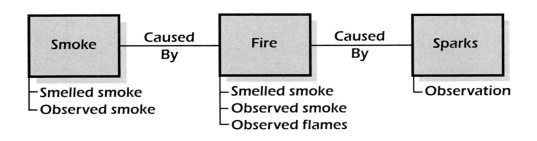

Watch the RealityCharting® Help Video titled "Evidence."

RealityCharting® automatically inserts a "?" in the evidence box.

# Acceptable Evidence Types

## Sensed Evidence

- Directly perceived by an individual
- Sight, Sound, Taste, Touch, Smell

## Inferred Evidence

- Known by repeatable causal relationships.
- Example: We know the pressure indicator reading is valid evidence of high pressure because we know the causes.
- Inferred evidence should always be verified.

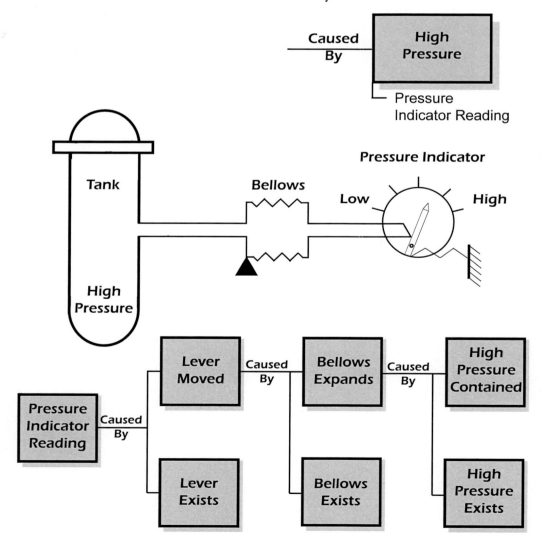

Apollonian Publications, LLC

# Exercise 4.3

## INSTRUCTIONS

Please review the Realitychart below to determine if all the evidence is acceptable or not.

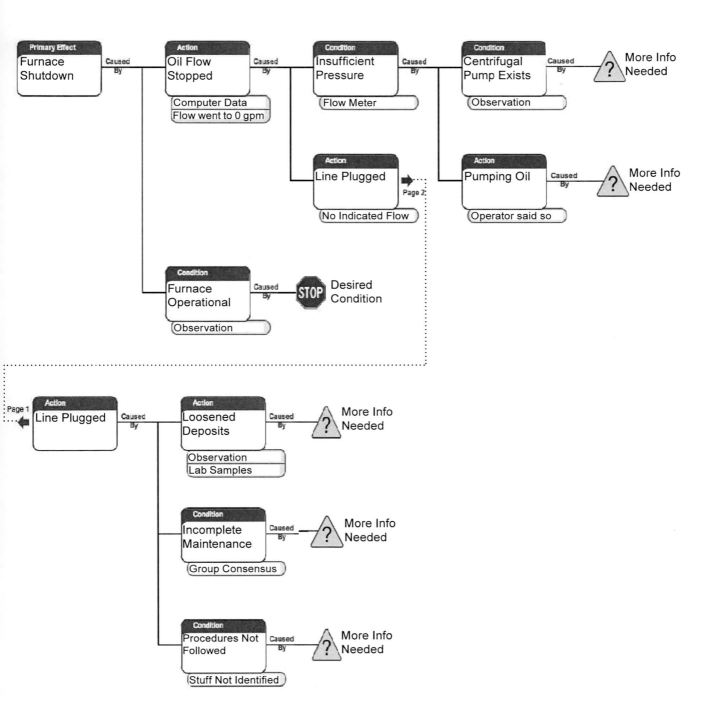

# Cause Path Endings
End Each Cause Path With "More Info Needed," a "Go To," Or A Reason For Stopping

## Cause Path Endings

- End all cause paths with one of the following
  - ◆ "More Info Needed"
    e.g.: Ask why until you don't have any answers. RealityCharting® provides this option and identifies this as an action item in the Action Items Report
  - ◆ "Desired Condition," meaning Desired Outcome or Situation
    e.g.: Met production goal, Procedure followed, Service level reached.
  - ◆ "Don't Have Control," if your next cause is outside your control.
    e.g.: Laws of physics, such as gravity or electricity.
  - ◆ "New Primary Effect," if the last cause is the beginning of another problem or separate analysis.
    e.g.: Material cracked; Fraud; Wrong software code.
  - ◆ "Other Cause Paths More Productive," if the cause path provides no value or return on investment.
    e.g.: Sky is blue.

## Feedback Loops

- Occasionally cause paths connect to established causes on your chart.
- RealityCharting® provides an easy way to link these causes using the "Go To" option in the node options menu.

 RealityCharting® uses a drop down menu to easily add reasons for stopping, More Info Needed, or a "Go To" feature that links the last cause in a chain to other causes already identified on your chart. It can also link to other Realitycharts so you can use several small charts to document a large analysis.

Apollonian Publications, LLC

# Two Phases of Realitycharting

## Phase 1: Creating The Draft Realitychart

- Assemble your team and use RealityCharting® and an overhead projector, or use a vertical surface for sticky notes.
- Ask for causes and document them on the chart or ask participants to write down causes and give to you.
- Use the Brainstorming feature in RealityCharting® to get started, or just start with the Primary Effect and begin asking why.
- If using the Brainstorming feature and the answers stop coming begin to create your Realitychart by asking why of the Primary Effect.
- Do not try to create the "right" Realitychart – no such thing.
- Use the Causal Elements view in RealityCharting® to help clarify the correct causal set.
- Iterate the chart until you reach your point of ignorance for each cause path.
- Use the Action Item Report created by RealityCharting® to identify missing causes and evidence.
- Go find missing data with further investigations and input results into RealityCharting®.

What is the right way to build a bridge? Answer: There isn't one right way, but you need to make it strong. The same is true of a Realitychart.

Watch the RealityCharting® Help Videos titled Refresher Training and Brainstorming.

# Two Phases of Realitycharting - Con't.

### Phase 2: Formalizing The Realitychart

- Use the RealityCharting® Wizard to complete your chart.
- Use a projector in a team meeting with key stakeholders.
- Go through the entire chart using the Causal Elements view to verify all the charting rules are met and evidence is presented.
- Run the Rules Check and Advanced Rules Check to verify proper chart structure.
- Share your chart with other stakeholders - Ask them to use the Track Changes feature to review and comment.
- Input their feedback and iterate the chart until all cause chains have been successfully ended.
- Finalize the report using Wizard Step 5.

 Watch the RealityCharting® Help Videos titled Wizard, Rules Check, and Track Changes.

Apollonian Publications, LLC

# Helpful Hints

## Identifying The Causes

- If you ask Why, and no answers come, look for causes in the following:
  - ♦ People; e.g.: Communications both written and oral, Performance both actual and intent, Personnel Statements
  - ♦ Procedures; e.g.: Regulations, Work Schedules, Policy Manuals, Design Drawings, Process Maps, Time Lines
  - ♦ Hardware; e.g.: Equipment Specifications, Installation Guides, Design Intent, Functional Application
  - ♦ Nature; e.g.: Ambient Conditions, Severe Weather, Laws of Physics
- Look for "what" is different and ask "why" it is different.
- Consider the function of a process, a component or a performance and ask if it met its intended function. If not, ask why and look for causes.
- Don't hesitate to go outside your group for more information.
- List possible causes even if no evidence exists. This will put them in the Action Items Report for further investigation.
- Email the Realitychart to your experts for help.

## Use Visual Aides

- Use process diagrams, schematics, organization charts, etc. to help everyone on the team understand the systems and configurations being evaluated.
- Use pictures, graphics, drawings, photographs and time lines to help everyone understand the problem.

Apollonian Publications, LLC

# More Helpful Hints

## Above All - Be Humble!

- The third principle of causation dictates that the more we know the more we know we don't know.
  - ◆ The last known cause on each cause path has at least two more causes.
  - ◆ There may also be causes between the known causes that we don't see.

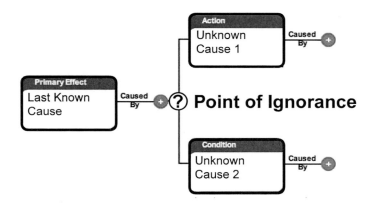

**The Structure of Humility**

"A wise man is a man who knows he knows not." - *Socrates.*

# Exercise 4.4
## Realitychart Development

**INSTRUCTIONS**

Work in a group of three to five people. Read the problem example described below, define the problem, and then build the Realitychart using RealityCharting® if you have access to it. Be prepared to discuss your findings as well as information you believe may be lacking.

## Introduction:

You are the Maintenance Manager at a small manufacturing facility. It is wintertime and a large bay door at the shipping dock is stuck in the partially open position. You have looked at the door and talked to the employees who work in the area. The following is what you know so far. The door rollers on one side are jammed in the track because two roller support brackets have failed while operating the door.

## Discussion With The Shipping Foreman:

"As you know, this problem has been around for about a year now. It started about a year after we installed this new track and roller type door. The door has always vibrated a lot, but I am not sure that is the problem. I think it is just part of the design and we need to do a better job of preventive maintenance. Why can't you guys just come in here and tighten the bolts every month or so. As you can see the bolts fall out. Here is one on the floor, right here – see it falls out when the door gets fully opened and the bolts get in a vertical position to fall out. The nuts have vibrated off so there is nothing to hold them in."

## Discussion With Maintenance Foreman:

"Yes, I have to replace those brackets quite often. It's no big deal because I keep a good supply of parts on hand and we have gotten real good at fixing the door. I can't fix it right now because it was one of the center support brackets and I don't have any of those in stock. But I called the door guys and they are sending some in overnight mail – be here tomorrow. Don't worry boss, we'll get this fixed up real soon. It's going to be a little cold in the shipping area tonight though."

Apollonian Publications, LLC

# Problem Definition

**What** _____

**When** _____

**Where** _____

**Significance**

    Safety _____

    Environment _____

    Revenue _____

    Cost _____

    Frequency _____

# Realitychart

**Primary Effect**

```
 _____
|                |      Caused
|                |------ _____
|                |        By
|_____|
```

# Realitychart Development
# (Exercise 4.4 continued)

### INSTRUCTIONS

Stay in your work group. Read the following information and add to your analysis. Be prepared to discuss your findings as well as information you believe may be lacking.

One day has passed and you have created your first draft Realitychart. You just came out of a morning meeting with the Plant Manager where you shared your Realitychart with him. You also showed him the following list of outstanding questions automatically created by RealityCharting's Action Item Report feature and asked for his support.

## Action Item Report

| Action Item | Name | Due Date |
| --- | --- | --- |
| Find out why No Preventive Maintenance | Maint. Mgr. | 5/8/12 |
| Find evidence for Bad Vibration | Resident Engineer | 5/12/12 |
| Find out why Bad Vibrations | Resident Engineer | 5/12/12 |
| Find out why Parts Not In Stock | Maint. Mgr. | 6/2/12 |

The Plant Manager has asked you to make this a number one priority because it has delayed shipping several critical orders.

**Discussion with Shipping Foreman:** "Well, we have confirmed that the new roller brackets have been shipped and they are coming in this morning on UPS. I guess the boss is upset about this problem, huh?" "I just started going through the Door Maintenance manual to see if I can find a minimum spare parts list. We've never set up a spares list for the doors, but you can be assured we will have these brackets in stock from now on."

**Discussion with the Resident Engineer:** (He was asked to look into this problem by the Plant Manager yesterday.) "I have been talking to your maintenance guys and they tell me there is no Preventive Maintenance performed on the shipping door. Why is that?"

**Maintenance Manager's Answer:** "Well, we've gotten pretty good at just fixing them when they break and it doesn't happen all the time. We just decided not to put this activity on the PM schedule. Besides we really didn't have any history on the door to warrant putting it on the PM schedule."

**Resident Engineer:** "Well, I have been looking into why the door vibrates so much and found that the door is inherently flexible by design – it just doesn't have enough cross bracing. Also, the main drive sprocket on this unit is the wrong one according to the manufacturer's Operation and Maintenance manuals. And, oh by the way, they recommend tightening the bracket bolts every month. I don't have any idea why they put the wrong sprocket on, but it is clearly their problem. This one does not align properly and it sets up a vibration in the drive belt, which then gets transferred into the door."

Apollonian Publications, LLC

## Problem Definition

**What** _____

**When** _____

**Where** _____

**Significance**

    Safety _____

    Environment _____

    Revenue _____

    Cost _____

    Frequency _____

## Realitychart

**Primary Effect**

```
┌─────────────────┐
│                 │_____  Caused
│                 │          By
│                 │_____
└─────────────────┘
```

Apollonian Publications, LLC

# Chapter 5
# Step 3: Identify Effective Solutions

"It is not the root causes we seek, it is effective solutions"
— *Dean L. Gano*

## Chapter Objectives

- Know the Criteria for Effective Solutions.
- Be Able to Apply the Creative Solutions Process.

Apollonian Publications, LLC

# Exercise 5.1
## What Makes A Solution Effective?

INSTRUCTIONS

Using some of the causes from Exercise 4.2, some possible solutions have been provided. Review each of these possible solutions and then write down a characteristic that makes it acceptable or not.

| Cause | Possible Solution | Reason for Accepting or Rejecting |
|---|---|---|
| Hinges failed | Replace hinges | |
| Wall vibrated | Mount cabinets on rubber shock absorbers | |
| First set screw missing | Replace and verify all set screws are in place and tight | |
| Gravity | Repeal gravity | |
| HVAC nearby | Move HVAC unit | |
| Door Exists | Remove doors | |

Apollonian Publications, LLC

# Solution Criteria

## Prevents Recurrence

- Prevents or mitigates this problem.
- Prevents similar problems.

## Within Your* Control

- Your control may be you, your department, your company, your suppliers or your customers.
- Nature is often not within your control.
- The facilitator is rarely the problem owner.

## Meets Your* Goals and Objectives

- The goals of the overall organization.
- The goals of your department or group.
- Your individual goals and objectives.
- Must provide reasonable value/ROI

## Does Not Cause Other Problems

- Must not cause other unacceptable problems that you are aware of.

Use RealityCharting® to document your solutions and check them against the solution criteria.

*Note

"Your" is the person or persons responsible for the success of the solution to prevent recurrence. Another common problem in many organizations is the failure of each employee to have a clear understanding of their goals and objectives. This may be a Primary Effect in itself.

# The Solutions Process
## How To Find Effective Solutions

**What is a solution?**

*An action taken upon a cause to effect a desired condition or outcome.*

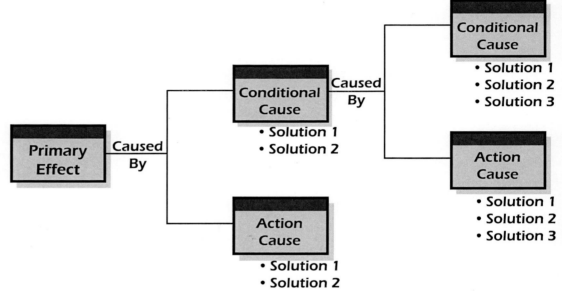

## Four Steps To Effective Solutions

1. Challenge each cause by asking how we can remove, change or control it.
2. Do not restrict any ideas, write down all possible ideas for each cause.
3. Check each solution against the solution criteria.
4. Implement the solutions that best pass the criteria.

Use RealityCharting® to check each solution against the solution criteria and use the Solution Assessment Report to prioritize solutions.

Apollonian Publications, LLC

# The Solutions Process
## Continued

### Challenge Each Cause And Offer Solutions

- RealityCharting® starts at the upper right side of the chart.
- Ask what can be done to remove, change or control the cause such that the primary effect does not recur.
- Write down every idea. Don't make judgments about solution effectiveness at this time.
- Offering solutions often causes you to see new causes; revise the chart.
- Be creative: go outside your box.

### Identify The Best Solutions

- They must meet the solution criteria:
    - ♦ Prevent recurrence.
    - ♦ Be within your control.
      Note: "Your control" may be your ability to influence others in control.
    - ♦ Meet your goals and objectives.
    - ♦ Not cause other problems that you are aware of.
- The best solutions are often applied to conditional causes.

### Process Interactions

- Use RealityCharting® Wizard Step 3 to challenge each cause on the chart.
- You may also find it helpful to use the Causal Elements View to challenge each cause in the causal sets.
- Or, print the chart and challenge each cause on the print out and offer solutions.
- Document your solutions in RealityCharting®.
- Run the Solutions Criteria Check.
- Identify which solutions you are going to implement.
- Identify who is responsible and when it will be completed.

Watch the RealityCharting® Help Videos titled Solutions - Wizard Step 3 and Solution Assessment Report.

Use the RealityCharting® solution generation tool (light bulb) to specifically place solutions. If you have a large number of causes to go through, this saves a lot of time.

# Solution Killers
Beware!

- It will never work here.
- We're too busy to do that.
- No one will buy it!
- We already tried that once.
- That's not our policy here.
- It isn't in the budget.
- Good thought, but impractical.
- Top management will never go for it.
- No one else is doing it that way.
- Wrong!
- We've always done it that way.
- Good idea, I'll get back to you - and never does.
- We will just be extra careful in the future.
- Add your own: _____

*Whether you think you can or think you can't –
you are right.*
*– Henry Ford*

# Helpful Hints

## Satisfying The Criteria

- In the course of identifying solutions, there may be some solutions that do not meet all criteria and still provide value. You may choose to implement them anyway, but make sure you identify them as supplemental solutions.

## Solutions Should Be Specific Actions

- Do not include solutions that are to be carried out in the future, such as Review..., or Analyze..., or Investigate. These are indicative of an incomplete problem analysis. If you choose to do this anyway, keep these solutions in a separate tracking log.
- Avoid solutions that include the prefix "re-," for example, retrain, re-read, replace.

Use RealityCharting "Advanced Find" feature to search for common causes.

## Look For The Systemic Solutions

- If you see recurring causes perhaps you have a systemic problem.

## The Solution May Be To Do Nothing

- Sometimes an effective solution cannot be found.
  - ◆ Cause & Effect relationships are not well known.
  - ◆ No cost effective solutions are developed: it is cheaper to live with the problem than solve it.
  - ◆ The causal set is unique, random or not likely to repeat itself.
- Sometimes there are no clear solutions. Devise a plan to capture more causal evidence if it happens again, and implement interim solutions that will mitigate the consequences.

Less than 0.6% of the US population does not understand the rules of society. The number of people who purposefully do not follow known rules is even less in the work place. (Based on the percentage of adults convicted of crimes and incarcerated in the USA.)

## Avoid Placing Blame

- If your solution is to punish or place blame, make sure it will prevent recurrence.

# Creative Solutions

## Be Creative

- Creativity requires the ability to escape the bonds of our own belief system.
- Challenge each cause.
- Think outside your group.

## Improve Your Thinking

- Discard the notions of a "right answer" or "common sense."
- Challenge conventional wisdom - it often holds us back.
- Challenge your own beliefs with an honest search for how you know what you think you know - understanding your ignorance opens the door to a new world of creative thought.
- Check your assumptions.
- Say: "I don't know." - then look elsewhere.
- Start with a really "far-out" solution and work with it until it is manageable, like "Only intelligent people are allowed to work here."

## Tapping Available Resources

- Use group synergy - when someone offers a solution, encourage discussion by saying: "Say more about that."
- Ask someone outside the group to look at your evaluation, and listen closely to their questions.

## Using Our Brains

- If you have the time, sleep on the problem - your subconscious mind works well at night.

Laughter is caused by improbable connections of two or more ideas. When brainstorming, listen for the laughter as it is the seeds of creative solutions.

Apollonian Publications, LLC

# Exercise 5.2
## Creative Solutions

### INSTRUCTIONS

Using your Realitychart from Exercise 4.4, challenge the causes and offer possible solutions using Wizard Step 3. Using the solution criteria, decide on the best solutions. The instructor will provide outside input and answer any questions you may have.

Before you move on to the next chapter, watch the RealityCharting® Help Videos titled Chart Navigation and Time Saving Features.

# Chapter 6
# Step 4: Implement & Track Solutions

*"Genius is the ability to put into effect what is on your mind."*
— *F. Scott Fitzgerald*

## Chapter Objectives

- Know the Key Elements of an Effective Event Report.
- Know How To Track Solutions.

Apollonian Publications, LLC

# Effective Communication
## Translating Gobbledegook Into Plain English

Over 200 years ago, opponents of Benjamin Franklin argued that a man should be required to own property before being allowed to vote. Franklin's supporters disagreed, and some of them stated their case as follows:

> "It cannot be adhered to with any reasonable degree of intellectual or moral certainty that the inalienable right man possesses to exercise his political preferences by employing his vote in referendums is rooted in anything other than man's own nature, and is therefore, properly called a natural right. To hold, for instance, that this natural right can be limited externally by making its exercise dependent on a prior condition of ownership of property, is to wrongly suppose that man's natural right to vote is somehow more inherent in and more dependent on the property of man than it is on the nature of man. It is obvious that such a belief is unreasonable, for it reverses the order of rights intended by nature."

Although Franklin agreed with this argument, he knew that people would not be convinced by such pompous oratory. So he chose to explain his position as follows:

> "To require property of voters leads us to this dilemma: I own a jackass; I can vote. The jackass dies; I cannot vote. Therefore the vote represents not me, but the jackass."

Always keep your report as simple as you can.

"If you can't say it simply, you probably don't understand it."
— *Albert Einstein*

Apollonian Publications, LLC

# Finalize the Report

- A well written and concise event report is required to document the corrective actions/solutions and the basis for these solutions - this is what RealityCharting® provides.
- A formal incident report should contain the following information as a minimum:
    - ◆ Problem Definition
    - ◆ Solutions, Action Items and Associated Causes
    - ◆ Responsible Person and Completion Date
    - ◆ Your Realitychart
    - ◆ Cost Information
    - ◆ Contact Name and Investigation Team Members
    - ◆ Report Date
    - ◆ Date Investigation Started
- Try to limit the report to one page.
    - ◆ Attach your Realitychart.

Writing a narrative of the event should be avoided because it invites storytelling, which invites politics and creates arguments. Using the Realitychart to communicate forces people to deal with the reality of the event.

Watch the RealityCharting® Help Video titled Incident Report.

RealityCharting® automatically creates key elements of the report and allows you to export it to any word processing document for further editing. You can also share the report by exporting it or creating a PDF.

# Implement Solutions

- Establish a Master Corrective Action Tracking Log
  - ◆ Frequent management review
  - ◆ If due date not met - Provide justification for failure
  - ◆ Failure to maintain discipline on this list will be seen as a lack of management commitment and the program will fail.
- Corrective actions should be agreed to and approved by those who have the authority and responsibility to implement them - no one else.
- Create a separate list for corrective actions that call for further review or study.

 If your organization has a formal action tracking system, make sure to input the action items from RealityCharting®.

Apollonian Publications, LLC

# Track Effectiveness

- Establish periodic reviews to evaluate solution effectiveness
- If corrective actions are ineffective redo the Realitychart
- Celebrate your successes by trending return on investment

Apollonian Publications, LLC

# Chapter 7
# Group Facilitation

"Working together to accomplish great things will always be part of the human experience, but success is dependent on individual courage to confront the group consensus."
    – *Paraphrased from GroupThink; CRM Films*

---

# Chapter Objectives

- Be Able to Facilitate an Incident Investigation.
- Understand the Common Traps.

Apollonian Publications, LLC

# Group Facilitation

## Be Familiar With the Realitycharting Process

- Know the structure of Realitycharts.
- Be comfortable with the fuzziness at the start.
- Always use RealityCharting® software to create your chart.
- Review the Facilitation Guidelines in Appendix A.

## Manage The Group

- Control group size; 5-6 is optimal, 8 max.
- For major problems you may need more than one team.
- Select stakeholders who know most about the event.
  - ♦ The team often changes as you learn more.
- Avoid too many supervisors/managers in group, unless key players.
- Don't use subject matter experts as facilitator - use an effective facilitator.
- Theme is prevention, not blame; don't stop at human error.
- Stick to the process.
- Realitychart creates a visual dialogue.
- Ask disruptive participants to let the process work - don't argue.
- Look for causes in emotional issues.

The best facilitator is often the one who knows least about the problem.

## Starting The Meeting

- Be comfortable with the ambiguity that will follow.
- Set the stage for an open climate.
  - ♦ e.g.: "We are here to find effective solutions, not go on a witch hunt."
- State the ground rules before you start.
  - ♦ See Facilitation Guidelines in Appendix A.

# Group Facilitation (continued)

## Facilitator's Responsibilities

- Keep team focused.
- Coordinate compilation of all Realitycharts.
- Compile report.
- Ensure team members complete their actions.
- Ensure solutions are assigned to those who have control.

## Performing The Analysis

- Suspend judgment of all input.
- Maintain a positive bias about all statements.
- Place all proposed causes on the chart - do not filter what is stated.
- Collect all the information the Realitychart requires.
- Put up a lot of causes.
- Don't skip the baby steps.
- If you can't place a cause ask "what did it cause?"

## The Realitychart Will Naturally Determine Value

- If a cause fits with others, it has value.
- If a cause has legitimate evidence it has value.
- All other causes will fall off the chart.

 Do Not filter stakeholder input - this kills the process. When building the chart, put all causes in the Holding area or on the chart, even if you don't know where they go - you can figure that out later.

Apollonian Publications, LLC

# Group Facilitation (continued)

## Appreciative Understanding Must Occur At Each Phase

- Problem Definition: List all stated primary effects.
- Realitycharting: List all stated causes.
- Creating Solutions: List all stated solutions.

## Solution Criteria Will Sort Out Most Effective Solutions

- Appreciate, but challenge Solution Killer statements.
- Appreciate who has control and include them in the problem-solving process.

## Review The Guidelines Listed Above Before Every Meeting

- Share appropriate ones with the team.

Go to the RC Learning Center and use Step 4 to practice your facilitation skills.

# Common Traps
## Obstacles To Group Facilitation

### Consensus

● Consensus is nothing more than an agreement to take a risk together. Voting on a root cause will not make it correct. Unfortunately, this is standard practice for the "Fishbone" process, and it ignores the reality of cause and effect. If the question is one of risk, or a "better" solution, then voting may be appropriate.

### Experts

● Experts are essential to effective problem solving, but always ask for evidence to support their information.
● If they state it is "their expert opinion," ask for examples of similar cause and effect relationships.
● If they cannot provide evidence, put a question mark below their causes.
● Avoid a contest of wills. Ask to be educated.

### Narrow-Minded Thinking

● Provincial or narrow minded thinking is perhaps the greatest barrier to creative solutions. Always go outside your team or group. The common belief is that if no one in the group knows the answer, then there is no answer. We then decide to stop asking why. As a facilitator, look for this. It is found in almost every team or group.

For more details on facilitation see Appendix A.

### Groupthink

● The condition of relinquishing our individuality for the common good of the group creates a condition called Groupthink. Look for it and mitigate it.

Apollonian Publications, LLC

# Review
## The Realitycharting Process

### 1.   Define the Problem

- Write down the following:
    - ♦ What – The Primary Effect
    - ♦ When
    - ♦ Where
    - ♦ Significance

### 2.   Create a Realitychart

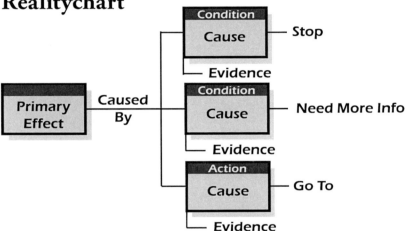

- For each effect ask "Why?"
- Look for causes in Actions & Conditions
- Connect causes with "Caused By"
- Support causes with Evidence or use a "?"
- End with a reason for stopping, Need More Info, or a Go To
- Run the Rules Check

### 3.   Identify Effective Solutions

- Challenge the causes and offer solutions
- Identify the best solutions - they must:
    - ♦ Prevent recurrence
    - ♦ Be within your control
    - ♦ Meet your goals and objectives
    - ♦ Not cause other problems you are aware of

When looking for actions and conditions it is common to find one action and two or more conditions.

### 4.   Implement and Track Solutions

Apollonian Publications, LLC

# Chapter 8
# Putting It All Together

"Success and failure follow the same cause path. The difference is that one is left to chance and the other is planned."
– *Dean L. Gano*

RT

## CHAPTER OBJECTIVES

- Root Cause Analysis Defined.
- Know How to Create an Effective Problem-Solving Culture.
- Review the Learning Objectives.
- Final Exam.

# Root Cause Analysis Defined

Root Cause Analysis is any structured process used to understand the causes of past events for the purpose of preventing recurrence. The results of this process must produce clear and concise documentation of all items listed below.

## An Effective Root Cause Analysis Process must:

Use these criteria to evaluate your current problem solving process.

1.  Define the problem to include the significance or consequence to the stakeholders
2.  Clearly delineate the known causal relationships that combined to cause the problem by providing a graphical representation of the causal relationships
3.  Clearly establish all causal relationships between the root causes and the defined problem as being necessary and sufficient
4.  Provide evidence to support each cause
5.  Identify and implement effective solutions
6.  Track and validate the effectiveness of the solutions

## Root Cause

Any cause in the cause continuum that is acted upon by a solution such that the problem does not recur. **It is not the root cause we seek, it is effective solutions.**

Caution: Categorical methods such as a Fishbone Diagram or so called "cause trees" that list predefined "causes" are hierarchical lists that do not provide legitimate causal relationships of the event. As such, effective solutions are questionable.

Apollonian Publications, LLC

# Effective Problem-Solving Culture - How To Easily Create One

Go to: www.realitycharting.com/training/comprehensive-plan

## Start At The Bottom

- Teach everyone the principles of causation with a 4-minute video. Go to http://www.realitycharting.com/methodology/principles and select the "What You Need To Know About Problem Solving" link. This one action on your part will do more to prevent problems in the first place.
- Make RC Simplified™ available to everyone so they can create their own Realitycharts of the small problems - no training required.
  - ◆ Fix small problems with RC Simplified™
- RC Simplified™ is part of the Effective Problem-Solving Culture Plan.

## Strengthen The Middle

- Stop arguing over how to fix a problem.
  - ◆ Use RealityCharting® to create a common reality that all stakeholders can buy into.
  - ◆ Use RealityCharting Coach™ and Facilitation Training to teach all managers, supervisors, and other key problem-solvers how to find effective solutions to major problems.
  - ◆ Go To: http://coach.realitycharting.com for online training.
- Create Problem-Solving Champions to facilitate major events and promote the problem-solving culture. For Details: http://www.realitycharting.com/training/problemsolvingculture/plan
- Create accredited facilitators for each business unit.

## Promotion From The Top

- Get management buy in and support.
  - ◆ Use free videos in the RC Learning Center™ to train all managers.
  - ◆ Deployment is easy with the RealityCharting Learning Center™.
  - ◆ Provide Return On Investment numbers for each solved problem.

# Implementation Plan
## The Details

### General Description

The following guidelines are provided to help organizations create an effective problem-solving culture. Please note that this is only a guide. Every organization is different, so before implementing this plan you should determine who the players are and what level of training they need. With our support, we can help you integrate the elements of this guide into your organization. This plan will be updated as we get your feedback on how to improve it, so please send your comments to us at www.realitycharting.com/contact-us.

### Critical Elements

To be effective, everyone in the work force:

1. Must be exposed to the principles of causation to understand that "stuff" does not just happen.
2. Should know that we can find effective solutions to event-based problems by using RealityCharting® and RC Simplified™.
3. Must understand that different perspectives are a key to effective solutions and easily accommodated when you use the Realitycharting process.
4. Must know their role in defining problems and finding effective solutions to prevent recurrence.
5. Must know that management is behind this initiative.

### Infrastructure

The following elements are required to implement this plan:

1. Top-level management support.
2. A Program Champion.
3. Dedicated Incident Investigation Facilitators.
4. Incorporation of the Realitycharting process into existing procedures and protocol.
5. Involve every employee in this effective problem-solving initiative.
6. Utilize RealityCharting®, the RC Learning Center™, and RC Simplified™ throughout the organization.

### Management Buy-in and Support

1. Show the Effective Problem-Solving video to top-level managers so they know the principles of effective problem-solving.
2. Show RealityCharting® Overview Video to all managers so they know what the software does and why it is so effective.
3. If they want to know more, managers should read the eBook: RealityCharting® – Seven Steps to Effective Problem Solving and Personal Success and work the interactive exercises in this book. To download, go to www.realitycharting.com/rcbook and enter the code DLG113. This is a pdf eBook that includes over 30 interactive links.

Apollonian Publications, LLC

# Plan - Continued

4. Provide a manager's workshop on Managing Effective Problem-Solving. Discuss application to Safety, Defect Elimination, Continuous Improvement programs such as Six Sigma, Lean, Proactive Maintenance, Chronic (Systemic) issues.

**Create A Program Champion**

1. Assignment
   a. The designated Program Champion can be developed with the help of our authorized training partners, or if a company already has an experienced incident investigator they may choose to be the Program Champion.
2. Qualifications:
   a. The Program Champion must be an experienced incident investigator and facilitator
   b. The Program Champion must have extensive knowledge of the latest version of RealityCharting® software and have completed the training program defined herein.
   c. The Program Champion should be an Accredited Facilitator.
3. Training:
   a. The Program Champion(s) must be familiar with the RealityCharting® learning tools to include the RC Learning Center™, RC Simplified™, and training videos, all of which can be accessed at http://coach.realitycharting.com/
   b. The Program Champion(s) must be a trained facilitator as defined in the Facilitator training below. If required, one of our training partners will provide expert guidance and training to help the Program Champion(s) become accredited.
   c. Program Champions should be mentored and certified by an authorized training partner. This should include being guided and mentored by the training consultant who may perform actual incident investigations to show the Program Champion trainee how it's done and then watch the Program Champion trainee facilitate actual events and mentor the trainee until they are deemed proficient.
   d. Required Reading: eBook: *RealityCharting – Seven Steps to Effective Problem Solving and Personal Success*. To download, go to www.realitycharting.com/rcbook and enter code DLG113.
4. Role of the Program Champion
   a. Mentor and be the "go to" person for all things relating to problem solving.
   b. Be able to effectively facilitate incident investigations.
   c. Incorporate problem-solving tools and techniques into the organization's procedures, such that everyone automatically knows what to do in the event of a problem.
   d. Present or facilitate the appropriate training to all stakeholders to make sure they know what to do when they see a problem.

  e. Create and maintain a set of Threshold Criteria that trigger formal incident investigations.

    i. Make sure everyone knows what the criteria are.

    ii. As fewer and fewer events trigger each criterion, lower its trigger point.

  f. Ensure all problem solutions are tracked to make sure they are implemented according to the approved schedule.

  g. Keep management informed of the status of all Threshold Criteria events, from the beginning of the investigation to the implementation of the solutions.

  h. Evaluate and trend the success of the solutions to prevent recurrence of all documented problems.

  i. Identify the savings generated from the non-repeat of events and calculate the Return On Investment of this initiative – present this information to management periodically.

  j. Evaluate all events for common cause using RealityCharting® Cause > Find Feature, or purchase RC Pro™ which provides unlimited data searches on all of your Realitycharts at the same time.

  k. Create Realitycharts for major successes and make sure all stakeholders know why they have been successful so they can continue to do the same things. This analysis may also identify weaknesses, risks, and serendipitous causal relationships – all of which can be strengthened.

### Audits

1. An annual audit of the program, investigation reports, skills, and success/failures should be performed by one of the authorized training partners to ensure quality of investigations, adherence to core principles of the RealityCharting Problem-Solving methodology, ensuring solutions are implemented and systemic problems identified.

### Dedicated Incident Investigation Facilitators

1. Identify Stakeholders

  a. Identify all stakeholders who have to solve problems as part of their daily work scope and train them. This usually includes the following:

    i. System or Process Engineers

    ii. Supervisors or Team Leaders

    iii. Some Managers

2. Training

  a. It is recommended that an authorized training partner provide training to the designated facilitators at the onset of this initiative. From this training the authorized training partner can provide recommendations, if needed, of which students show the most promise of being a good Program Champion.

  b. Facilitation training shall consist of each student installing RealityCharting® software and using RC Coach™ to learn the process and the software. If any questions arise during this training, they can contact the training consultant and get answers, or the consultant may choose to kick off the training with an online conference and use that as a forum to complete this part of the training.

  c. Facilitator students will work at least two Facilitation Simulator exercises in the RealityCharting Learning Center™ and use RealityCharting® software to create at least two charts of real problems of their own. They should try to collaborate with one or two other trainees for this exercise. The training consultant will review them to ensure they are done properly and provide feedback as needed.

3. Mentoring Process
   a. The Program Champion should mentor other practitioners and support other practitioners to develop their skills for conducting more complex investigations by encouraging them to become accredited.
   b. Note: By encouraging facilitators to continuously improve their problem solving skills you not only embed this thinking into the culture, it creates a line of succession if the Program Champion leaves.

## Integration

Incorporate the RealityCharting® problem-solving tools and training into the existing company procedures and protocols as follows:
1. Entry Points
   a. Identify problem-solving entry points by reviewing the work processes.
      i. Problems can occur anywhere and this evaluation should include what the actions of any employee should be if they identify a problem.
      ii. This may include Non-Conformance Reports, Corrective Action Reports, and Customer Feedback Forms.
2. Minor Problems
   a. If the problem is below the threshold criteria for performing a full-blown ARCA™, employees should use RC Simplified™ to document the problem as they see it and send the Realitychart to their Supervisor/Team Leader and the Program Champion.
3. Getting Help
   a. If an employee is not capable of using RC Simplified™ for whatever reason, they should go to their Team Leader, supervisor, or other designated person who does have access and work with them to do the first cut analysis.
4. Problem Identification Form
   a. If none of the above will work, the employee should fill out a designated problem identification form and give it to their Team Leader/Supervisor. The form should simply ask them to describe the problem as they see it – this entry point must be simple. Working with the stakeholders involved, the supervisor can then use RC Simplified™ or RealityCharting® to analyze the event.

## General Employee Training

1. Watch Video
   a. As a minimum all employees should watch the 4-minute "What You Should Know About Problem Solving" video, but the 17-minute Effective Problem Solving video should also be viewed. If possible the Program Champion should be present when watching and answer any questions people may have. The Program Champion may want to stop it at certain points and add examples that are applicable to the business. This can be

part of the introduction to the effective problem-solving initiative or general employee training.

2. Use RC Simplified™
   a. RC Simplified™ is an excellent training tool in addition to an entry-level problem-solving tool. If employees have access to a computer and the web, show them RC Simplified™ and ask them to view the training videos provided in the Help menu of RC Simplified™ and then ask them to create and submit a problem analysis of any problem they may be having now. It can be company related or not. These should be submitted to the Program Champion for review, information and to provide feedback to the individuals to help them understand the principles of causation.

## Implementation Strategies

1. Initial Findings
   a. If the initial problem analysis using RC Simplified™ provides effective solutions, then implement them according to existing procedures and approval protocol.
      i. Send the final analysis to the Program Champion for review and approval and put into the organizations tracking and trending system and/or print, or otherwise transmit the final copy to stakeholders who may need it.
      ii. The Program Champion will review to determine if the problem exceeds the threshold criteria for a formal investigation and respond accordingly. He/she shall also convert the simplified chart to a Realitychart and put it in the database for common cause review using RC Pro™.
      iii. This protocol provides the Program Champion oversight of how well the program is working and when and where to adjust it.
2. Incomplete Analysis
   a. If the event-analysis using RC Simplified™ does not find effective solutions, then send the initial Realitychart to the Program Champion.
      i. The Program Champion will determine if the problem exceeds the threshold criteria for a formal investigation and respond accordingly.
      ii. The Program Champion will determine if he/she can finish the analysis or if a team is needed to work the issue.
      iii. If a team is required, the Program Champion will gather the team and work with them to finalize the analysis. The Program Champion may lead the analysis or ask their authorized ARCA™ consultant to do it. This is usually a function of the size of the organization and the functional domain.

## Deployment

1. Roll Out
   a. Depending on the size of the organization it may be necessary to roll this initiative out in a stepwise fashion.
      i. You may want to start with one business unit or discipline and as you work the kinks out move to another unit or discipline, until full deployment is achieved.
2. Ease of Deployment
   a. Deployment is easy because the RC Learning Center™ is a web-based training platform.
      i. Use the RealityCharting Learning Center™ to access the free videos and other teaching aids as required.
      ii. Use the Exercises (Step 4) in the RC Learning Center™ to work real-world events and create a Realitychart. If you have problem examples that are specific to your business that you want added to this feature, send them to Realitycharting (www.realitycharting.com/contact-us) and we will add them. We can remove any sensitive information to make them look generic.

# Learning Objectives Review

1. What are the steps to an effective problem analysis?
2. What are the key elements of a problem statement?
3. What do the cause and effect principles tell us?
4. How do you ensure an effective problem analysis?
5. What makes an effective solution?
6. Where do you find root causes?
7. How do you find creative solutions?
8. What are the key elements of an event report?
9. Why is it not a good idea to include a narrative in an event report?
10. After implementing a solution, what's next?
11. Where can you practice facilitating an event?
12. How does RealityCharting® automatically create an Action Item Report?
13. How do you ensure institutionalization of effective problem solving?
14. What feature in RealityCharting® allows you obtain and review feedback from other stakeholders?
15. If you are using RealityCharting® and want to learn more about a certain feature, what should you do?
16. What type of cause is "Incomplete Procedure?"
17. What Page Layout View should you use to iterate and create your chart?
18. In RealityCharting® what is required to complete the Identify Solutions Step?
19. Which of these causes could be followed by a cause path ending of "Desired Condition?" a. Procedure Completed b. Seal Exists c. Flange Seal Failure d. Procedure Exists.
20. What tools are provided for you to easily institute an effective problem-solving culture?

Apollonian Publications, LLC

# Continuous Improvement

**To**: Students

**From**: Dean L. Gano
**Subject**: Learning

Congratulations on completing this course. Like any new knowledge, you must use it to appreciate what it can do for you. For those who use it, you will be rewarded with a significant return on investment. In the twenty plus years we have been teaching this process, those who "get it" go on to become highly successful. Common success headlines are "Employee of the Year," "Making lots of money," "In high demand," "Improved the way I look at life." In one case the result was saving a large well known manufacturing company from bankruptcy.

Learning requires interaction, appreciative understanding and integration of new information. If we can agree that the Realitycharting problem-solving tools you just learned through class interaction are simple and valuable, then you have the first two elements of learning behind you. All you need now is to integrate this new knowledge into your daily activities.

To make it easier for you to integrate this new knowledge, we have created RealityCharting® software and the RealityCharting Learning Center™. Using RealityCharting® is like having an instructor on your shoulder guiding you through the process so what you learned in class is reinforced each time. If you can't remember something about the software open a help video. If you can't remember something about the process, go to the Help menu in RealityCharting®, open the RealityCharting Learning Center™ and go to RC Coach™.

To begin the next step in the learning process, please find a problem in your world and apply what you learned in class. If possible, do this with others who have recently been trained. Use RealityCharting® to guide you, share information, and document your findings. After completing at least two Realitycharts, go take the Investigator Accreditation Exam and become accredited. In time, get your Facilitator Accreditation. Talk to your instructor to learn more.

Be a force for change in your organization by promoting the effective problem-solving culture plan and sharing what you have learned with others. Continue to use RealityCharting® on all your significant events. As your new solutions become much more effective and easier to implement than your old favorite solutions, you will never go back to the old ways, and integration will be complete.

# Accreditation

## Become an Accredited RealityCharting® Investigator:

1. Complete this classroom training or RC Coach™.
2. Successfully complete a 50 question written exam with questions randomly chosen from a 100-question database. - Passing grade is 80%.
3. Analyze an event and submit a Realitychart for review. Must meet all requirements of an effective analysis to pass
4. Upon successful completion, receive an Exclusive ARCA™ Accreditation Certificate from Applonian Publications, LLC.
5. If you choose, your name will be added to our list of Accredited Investigators, available on our web site, or you can remain anonymous.
6. Exam and accreditation created and overseen by Dean L. Gano; creator and owner of the Realitycharting process.
7. To learn more contact your instructor/provider or go to www.realitycharting.com/accreditation.

## Become an Accredited RealityCharting® Facilitator:

1. Pre-requisite: Be an accredited RealityCharting® Investigator.
2. Successfully complete a comprehensive 100 question written exam with questions randomly chosen from a 200-question database. - Passing grade is 80%.
3. Certify that you have facilitated at least 10 incident investigations using RealityCharting®.
4. Facilitate a real world investigation under the tutalage of an Accredited Instructor or Program Champion.
5. Upon successful completion receive an Exclusive ARCA™ Accreditation from Appolonian Publications, LLC.
6. If you choose, your name will be added to our list of Accredited Facilitators, available on our web site, or you can remain anonymous.
7. Exam and accreditation created and overseen by Dean L. Gano; creator and owner of the Realitycharting process.
8. To learn more contact your instructor/provider or go to www.realitycharting.com/accreditation.

Apollonian Publications, LLC

# A Note on Accreditation

Reality Charting® also known as Apollo Root Cause Analysis has been taught to well over 100,000 people worldwide in eleven different languages for more than two decades. It has become known as the premier RCA methodology and is used by many of the fortune 500 companies and government agencies like the FAA and NASA.

By becoming an accredited Investigator or Facilitator, you will become part of an elite group who have taken this training to a higher level proving your understanding and dedication to effective problem solving. As such an individual you provide greater value not only to yourself, but to those you work with or for. As discussed early on in this training manual, those who have taken what they learned here to the next level have become very successful in their jobs and indeed in their lives as a whole.

We regularly get calls from employers who are looking for someone who is "certified" in RealityCharting®. Many companies require knowledge in RealityCharting® for various positions, so you will be in demand no matter where you work. Moreover, the single most important job skill employers ask for is "good problem solving skills." Since we are not taught that in school you are left to your own devices and maybe your are good or maybe you are not, but with a RealityCharting® accreditation you can show your employer that you have the skills they require to be an effective problem solver.

To learn more, go to www.realitycharting.com/accreditation.

Apollonian Publications, LLC

# Appendix A
# Facilitation Guidelines

# Appendix A: Facilitation Guidelines

Apollonian Publications, LLC

# Introduction

Problem solving is a way of thinking, not a procedure. Therefore, it is with great trepidation that we provide the following guidelines. As tempting as it might be, please do not use the following information to create a procedure. To do so is to get rule-based thinking confused with cause and effect thinking. These are only guidelines to be used to get the novice started. As you gain confidence and experience, you will find what works for you. Remember, there are only four steps in the RealityCharting process, and RealityCharting® will guide you through each one.

## 1. Gather Information (See Appendix B for More Details)

a. Gathering information is a continual process starting with finding out everything you can about the problem and continuing until you verify that the solution meets the solution criteria. Gathering information is not an individual task. Everyone in the organization should be trained and understand the need for causes and evidence. If they have not been trained, the facilitator should always give a short explanation at the beginning of the first team meeting or require them to watch the *Effective Problem Solving* video found in the RealityCharting Learning Center™ before attending the meeting.

b. Any narrow minded judgments or biases used to filter or eliminate information at this stage may prove very damaging to your success later on - do not discard anything.

c. Establish and follow a policy that quarantines the event area and requires collection of evidence if applicable.

d. Establish an evidence preservation checklist and follow it. Refer to Chapter 12 of the companion book: *RealityCharting® - Seven Steps to Effective Problem-Solving And Strategies For Personal Success* for an example checklist.

e. Ask everyone involved with the event to provide information on what they were doing at the time, what they heard, saw or sensed in any way. A simple form works well, or if time permits, interview each person involved.

f. Based on the initial information and problem definition, the facilitator should determine who will be involved in the problem-solving team. NOTE: This may change as more information becomes available. Only invite people who will contribute to the effort.
Caution: Limit the number of people in the team to 7 or 8. Four or five is optimal for most events. With a very complicated problem, you may want to create multiple teams to address special areas. These teams should report to the main team by providing their Realitychart to the Team leader [it is easily imported into the master chart]. Maintain a master Realitychart that is always available to team members.

g. Develop a sequence of events or time line before you do a Realitychart. The sequence of events will provide an initial set of action causes that can be placed into a Realitychart. Since time lines are a story, avoid story telling in your cause boxes.

h. Utilize input from RC Simplified™ charts. This can occur if someone has tried to solve the problem with RC Simplified™ and found the problem to be too complex for RC Simplified™, or you may ask team members who are not qualified to use RealityCharting to use RC Simplified™ to provide what they see as the problem. Note: RC Simplified™ does not require any formal training.

# Appendix A: Facilitation Guidelines

## 2. Define The Problem

a. After gathering the initial information, the team should come together with an overhead projector to display RealityCharting® and any other relevant information, like the ground rules.

b. Open the meeting with your expectations and set ground rules:
   1. Purpose is to fix the problem, not the blame.
   2. Everyone is here to contribute.
   3. This is an open dialogue, no judging or stating conclusions until the solutions phase.
   4. We are not trying to find the right answer, we are going to find the best solutions.
   5. We will not talk about solutions until after we create a Realitychart.
   6. The best solutions must meet the solution criteria.
   7. Be patient with the process.
   8. No side conversations.
   9. We are looking for causes and their supporting evidence.
   10. Everything is open to discussion, but the facilitator reserves the right to direct the discussion to follow evidence based causes.
   11. Assumptions are encouraged, and they will be labeled with a question mark until we can find supporting evidence.

c. Begin to define the problem by asking the team members to identify the Primary Effect (PE).

d. Record every possible cause using the Brainstorming feature in RealityCharting®. Encourage an open dialogue. No one judges, and remind anyone who does of the ground rules. It is not unusual to feel you have lost control at this stage. This is quite normal, and can last for 20-30 minutes. You are experiencing an outpouring of each individual reality, and it is usually productive as long as everyone follows the ground rules. Listen very carefully and document every cause you hear without regard for where it fits into the puzzle. Remember causes are noun-verb phrases so listen for them. To keep everyone interested, try to validate their ideas by placing their causes on the chart or in the Holding Area.

f. After you have a general agreement on the primary effect, finish the problem statement by writing the When, Where, and Significance so everyone can see. Remember to provide specific information about safety, cost, frequency, etc.

g. Try not to proceed until every member agrees with the written problem statement. If you cannot get concurrence, remind dissenters that this can be changed anytime, and ask if you can move on.

h. If there is more than one Primary Effect, write out a problem statement for each, and then proceed to ask "why," one Primary Effect at a time.

Apollonian Publications, LLC

# 3. Create A Realitychart

Creating a Realitychart is a two phase process. Phase one creates a draft Realitychart. Phase two formalizes and finishes your Root Cause Analysis using RealityCharting® software.

### *Phase One: Creating the Draft Realitychart*

a. Starting with the Primary Effect, begin asking why or asking "caused by?" until you no longer get answers. If you utilized the Brainstorming feature to gather causes, place them on the chart in their proper order.

b. Don't try to define the actions and conditions at this time - just put the causes in order on the chart.

c. Minimize discussion at this time by asking "why" immediately after placing the cause on the chart. This is an important point in the process because it keeps people focused and keeps you moving down a productive path. Anything you can do to keep moving prevents story telling and gets you to a common reality much sooner. Minimizing the drudgery of an investigation causes people to want to do this again on other problems.

d. Go back to the Primary Effect (Square One) and start through the cause chains again.

e. This time through, look for causes in actions and conditions in each causal set. Use the Causal Elements view to focus on causal sets.
   **Caution:** Remember, the reason you are looking for actions and conditions is that theoretically you know they are there and you want as many opportunities for solutions as possible. Do not get bogged down in actions and conditions, especially on the first time through the square one loop. Ideas and causes are usually coming so fast on the first pass, it is better to keep the momentum going than to slow down the thought process by labeling causes. As you go through the second and subsequent loops, look for more branches and baby steps. And Remember that if you have an action cause you can easily state an associated conditional cause simply by adding the verb "Exists" to the Noun in the Action cause.

Always use RealityCharting® with an overhead projector so you can see the big picture.

f. Repeat the square one loop as many times as you need to get to your point of ignorance or a decision to stop at the end of each cause chain.

g. Complete the Realitychart as best you can with the limited knowledge you have. Remember it is impossible to know all the causes. Problem significance will help you to know how far to go with baby steps or termination of the chains. Time may also cause you to limit exploration. Your purpose is to find creative solutions that meet your goals and objectives, and if you accomplish that, then you have accomplished what you set out to do. When you get to the solutions stage and you cannot find an effective solution, then work on the chart some more.

h. If story telling erupts, let it go as long as you are getting causes out of the story, but as soon as it digresses into who did what at such-n-such a time at such-n-such a place, stop it, and get back into the square one loop.

i. Use the Action Item Report created by RealityCharting® to identify missing causes and evidence. Go find missing data with further investigations and input results into RealityCharting®.

# Appendix A: Facilitation Guidelines

  j. Make sure not to stop too soon on each cause path. Make sure your reason for stopping is a legitimate one. Reasons for stopping are: desired condition, lack of control, new primary effect, other cause paths more productive, or more info needed. The most common tendency is to stop at categorical causes like "Training Less Than Adequate (LTA)," or "Maintenance LTA." Another common stopping point is "Procedures Not Followed." These are categories, not causes, and they must be explained in more detail. Sometimes it helps to ask, "What do you mean by LTA or Not Followed?"

  k. Refrain from discussing solutions and "Root Causes" while you are constructing the Realitychart.

### Phase Two: Finishing and Formalizing the Realitychart

From this point on, group facilitation will be accomplished by meetings as needed for discussion and electronic communications using RealityCharting® and other common software tools.

  a. Use the RealityCharting® Wizard to complete your chart.

  b. Share your Realitychart with other stakeholders and ask for input using the Track Changes feature. Identify all unknown causes with a question mark in the evidence box or use the More Information Needed option in the node menu. This will automatically generate an Action in the Action Item Report.

  c. Open the Action Item Report in the Reports menu and assign responsibilities and due dates. Distribute the Action Item Report as required.

  d. As the action items complete, update the Realitychart and send the new version out to the stakeholders for review and comment.

  e. Continue to input your findings and iterate the chart until all cause chains have been successfully ended.

  f. Go through the entire chart using the Causal Elements view to verify all the charting rules are met and evidence is presented.

  g. Run the Rules Check and Advanced Rules Check to verify proper chart structure.

Apollonian Publications, LLC

## 4.   Identify Solutions

a.   Once you have decided to stop adding causes to your chart and you have completed Step 2 in RealityCharting®, either print the chart or use an overhead screen and brainstorm solutions with all key stakeholders. This can be done electronically or in a meeting. The meeting forum works best if possible because it allows for synergy.

b.   As you challenge each cause, provide solutions. Do not be concerned about strict compliance with the solution criteria at this time, but keep in mind not to be completely ridiculous. This is similar to brainstorming in the sense that you should allow unbiased free-thought. However, there is structure because you are focused on the control or removal of a cause. Get all team members involved in the creative solutions process to build ownership. **Note**: As you gain experience with the RealityCharting process, you will find the solution criteria are part of your thinking as you go through each square one loop. While it should not restrict your thinking, it acts as a guide to keep you focused on a solution that prevents recurrence, is within your control, meets your goals and objectives and does not cause other problems.

c.   Utilize Wizard Step 3 to challenge each cause and propose possible solutions. Do not waste time with causes that do not offer good solutions. If no one in the group can think of anything, then move on. Normally, this should not take more than 20 minutes as a group activity. If you have time, it is a good idea to let the solutions "cook" for some time, and let the team members think a little further about the possibilities. Talk with people outside the group about the proposed solutions, or go to the place where the solution will be implemented, and try to visualize implementation. This often identifies other problems that might be created.

d.   Be very careful not to stop with your favorite solution or a group consensus that compromises the effectiveness of the best solution.

e.   After you have entered all your possible solutions into RealityCharting® use it to verify compliance with the solution criteria.

f.   Select which solutions you plan to implement.

g.   Select Wizard Step 4 and finish the report.

## 5.   Finalize the Report

a.   Using RealityCharting®, finalize your analysis by selecting Wizard Step 5; Finalize Report.

b.   Send the finalized report to all stakeholders for review and approval. If you get comments at this stage, remember that you do not have to be defensive about what you created. If someone has new perspectives and evidenced based-causes to add, put them on the chart – it's easy and they may lead to better solutions. One of the greatest values of using the Realitycharting process is that its core value is to create a common reality that everyone can understand and buy into. By its very nature, creating a common reality in your Realitychart assures the best solutions.

Apollonian Publications, LLC

# Appendix B
# Gathering Data

"Everything should be as simple as possible; but not simpler."
– *Albert Einstein*

Apollonian Publications, LLC

# Collecting Information

## Understanding the Event

- Respond promptly
    - ◆ The further in time we move from event initiation, the less detail we are likely to know about the event.
    - ◆ Establishing Threshold Criteria helps us to move quickly on critical events.
- Develop a time-line
    - ◆ A sequence of events may be important to understanding the causation of the event.
    - ◆ Understand relativity, if any, in the event timing.
- Get the story
    - ◆ Identify people that may have insight to the event and allow communication in a story format.
    - ◆ Listen for causes in the "story" and ask "causal" questions.
    - ◆ Consider the event functionally and identify specialists and experts that know and understand the conditional infrastructure.

## Group Dynamics

- Serious events may be emotionally charged.
    - ◆ Consider the mood or sensitivities of the group when interviewing people.
    - ◆ It may be helpful to know the groups goals and objectives relative to the event analysis.
    - ◆ Always attempt to collect information as close to the source of cause as possible.
    - ◆ If possible, wait for emotions to wane before asking why.

# Evidence Gathering & Preservation

## Sources of Evidence

- Evidence may be found in people, procedures, hardware and nature.
- Always secure the environment until evidence and data are gathered.
- What was the location of people or components.
- What tools or equipment were used.
- What procedures, laws or work practices were applicable.
- Personal testimony.
- Failed parts or equipment.
- Computer printouts or transient data.

## Preservation of Evidence: No Contamination

- Document the event environment with photos, sketches or process maps.
- Do not touch fractured surfaces; get them to a material specialist ASAP.
- Preserve the condition of failed hardware; the condition of the hardware may provide an important insight to causation.

## Quality of Evidence

- Sensed evidence is the most reliable; it is seen, heard, tasted, touched or smelled.
- Inferred evidence may need to be verified; instrument and indicator readings are all inferred until verification occurs.
- Allow event significance to determine the need for verification.

Apollonian Publications, LLC

# Introduction to Interviews

The following is a collection of interview information from many sources to include students like you, so if you have anything to add at the end of this section, please share it with the class. Some of these ideas may be effective for you, some may not. Use them accordingly.

## Purpose:

To gather information to be used in defining a historical action or event.

## An Interview is *Not*:

- An inquisition
- An effort to find fault
- An effort to place blame
- Just a friendly chat

## An Interview *Should Be*:

- A well planned dialogue
- An effort to find the facts
- 70% listening, 30% asking and explaining

## Communication Is:

- 60% nonverbal (body language)
- 30% tonal (voice)
- 10% from the spoken word

The key to effective interviewing is listening.

# Interview Prerequisites

- Interviewee must have an incentive to participate.
    - ◆ Help solve a problem (fulfill need to be needed).
    - ◆ Gain approval or acceptance of beliefs.
    - ◆ Need to learn.
    - ◆ No incentive if punishment is a consequence.
- Interviewer must have credibility with interviewee.
- If trust is lacking, include a neutral third party in the interview.
- Must have a clear purpose for the interview, and be able to state it.
- Understand the group dynamics prior to the interview.
- Must have predefined questions.
- Must be prepared to listen with an open mind.
- Dress accordingly.
- Provide agenda or list of questions (if appropriate) prior to interview.
- Catch people at a relaxed time in their schedule.

 Everyone has the need to be needed. Some say it is the strongest need humans have. Use it to get good information from the interviewee by being the student.

Apollonian Publications, LLC

# The Interview Process

Before you start an interview, always review these guidelines to refresh your mind and prepare by visualizing how you will do the things discussed in this section.

# Part 1: Setting The Stage

- Always meet on the turf of the interviewee or a neutral location.
- Sit on the same side of the table.
- Ensuring success with a difficult interviewee.
    - ◆ For the hostile interviewee, have someone they respect* perform the interview; you can collaborate on purpose and specific questions.
    - ◆ For the impatient interviewee ask their supervisor to schedule the time and remind them of the importance.
    - ◆ For the apathetic interviewee, have someone they respect* perform the interview; collaborate on purpose and specific questions.
    - ◆ For the suspicious interviewee, have the interviewee and another person, such as a Union Representative present.

* If there is no such person, use the "need to be needed" philosophy. Start by asking for honest opinions and listen without rebuttal, and then work your way to predefined questions.

Apollonian Publications, LLC

# Part 2: Starting The Interview

- Explain purpose or goal of the interview, and ask if the interviewee feels comfortable with sharing information.
- Communicate the common goal you both have.
    - ◆ Preventing the problem from recurring
    - ◆ Meeting customers needs, etc.
- Give background and what facts you know at present.
- Let interviewee know that their name will not appear in any reports.
- Give estimated duration of interview.
- Start questioning with open ended questions:
    - ◆ "Please help me to understand what happened."
    - ◆ "What would you do differently?"
- Use open ended questions whenever you think you are dominating the conversation i.e. "Teach me."
- Don't be afraid to let them know you are capable of making mistakes.

# Part 3: The Interview

- Stick with your prepared questions, but don't jump right into them; let interviewee "warm up" first.
- Ask for "feelings", opinions and "facts", as well as solutions. They can help you understand the organizational culture.
- Keep on track with prepared questions, but encourage all relevant discussion. For example, "go on" or "and what does that mean to you?"
- Always be honest; if you don't know, say so.
- Use "dead air" or a long pause after a question to give the interviewee time to think.
- Concentrate on the "You" of the interview and ask questions as if you are a student and the interviewee is the expert teacher. For example, "I don't understand, could you elaborate?"
- Maintain eye contact as much as possible to pick up on nonverbal communication.
- Be enthusiastic about answers.
- Take good notes, or have someone else take them.
- Think cause and effect.
- Listening is the key.
    - We talk at approximately 125 words per minute and listen (receive) at approximately 400 to 600 words per minute.
    - Concentrate on listening, evaluating logic, understanding and determining accuracy (don't prejudge, or argue).
    - Listen for content, emotion and relative value and try to paraphrase these three things or make note of them.

Apollonian Publications, LLC

# Part 4: Closing

- Give a brief review of how helpful the interviewee has been.
- Tell what will be done with the information. Give credit where credit is due.
- Promise to give feedback and be specific if you can. e.g.: "I will send you a copy of the final report."
- Never pass up a chance to say thank you. Be genuine.
- Ask if there are any questions.
- Review highlights of your notes, and ask interviewee if your notes are correct.
- Ask person to call you if they think of any relevant information in the next day or two.
- Ask for referrals.
- Ask if there is anything they expected you to ask but didn't.

Apollonian Publications, LLC

# Appendix C
# References

Apollonian Publications, LLC

# References

1. Gano, Dean L., 2011, RealityCharting® - Seven Steps To Effective Problem-Solving And Strategies for Personal Success, Apollonian Publications, LLC, Richland, WA, ISBN 978-1--883677-13-8

2. Gano, Dean L., August 1987, Root Cause and How to Find it, Nuclear News, pp 39-43.

3. Gano, Dean L., November, 1994, Total Failure Management, Quality Digest, pp 56

4. Covey, Stephen R., 1989, The Seven Habits of Highly Effective People, Simon & Schuster Fireside Books, ISBN 0-671-70863-5.

5. Gano, Dean L. October, 2003, Problem Solving Revisited, ARMS Reliability Conference Papers, 2003, Victoria, Australia

7. Covey, Stephen R., 1990, Principle-Centered Leadership, Simon & Schuster Summit Books, ISBN 0-671-74910-2

8. De Bono, Edward, 1992, Serious Creativity, Harper Business, ISBN 0-88730-566-0

9. Van Doren, Charles, 1991, A History of Knowledge, Ballantine Books, ISBN 0-345-37316-2

10. Senge, Peter, 1990, The Fifth Discipline, Currency Doubleday, ISBN 0-305-26095-4

11. Damasio, Antonio, 1994, Descartes' Error, Grosset/Putnam, ISBN 0-399-13894-3

12. "Groupthink," CRM Films, Phone: 1-800-421-0833

13. Goleman, Daniel, 1995, Emotional Intelligence, Bantam Books, ISBN 0-553-09503-X

14. Guidelines for Hazard Evaluation Procedures, 1990, American Institute of Chemical Engineers, ISBN 0-671-74910-2

15. Hussey, Dennis, 1999, Measuring Problem Solving Effectiveness, American Society of Safety Engineers Professional Development Conference, page 361

16. Carter, Rita, 1999, Mapping The Mind, University of Calif. Press, Berkeley, CA, ISBN 0-520-22461-2

Apollonian Publications, LLC

# Appendix D
# Glossary

Apollonian Publications, LLC

# Glossary

## ACTIONS

Causes that interact with conditions to cause an effect. Sometimes called *action causes*.

## APPRECIATIVE UNDERSTANDING

A prerequisite mind-set for effective problem solving that is characterized by suspending judgement and maintaining a positive attitude. It occurs by accepting all incoming information at face value and allowing the RealityCharting RCA technique to determine value.

## BABY STEPS

Causes between the causes that represent a finer look at causal relationships. All causal relationships have causes between the causes, we are typically just too ignorant to see them.

## CATEGORICAL THINKING

The natural process of the mind that orders all knowledge into specifically defined classes. It can present a significant barrier to effective problem solving.

## COMMON REALITY

A combined reality created from the individual realities of several people and documented by a Realitychart. If an individual's reality does not fit into the common reality, it is likely because the person can not provide causal evidence, or their point of view is seeing a different problem.

## COMMON SENSE

The common feeling of humanity. Common sense is an illusion that causes ineffective problem solving.

## CONDITIONS

Causes that exist in time prior to an action bringing them together to cause an effect. Sometimes called conditional causes.

## EFFECTIVE PROBLEM SOLVING

Identifying causal relationships and controlling one or more of the causes to affect the problem in a way that meets our goals and objectives. A key goal of event-based problems is to prevent recurrence.

## EFFECTIVE SOLUTION

A solution that prevents problem recurrence.

## ELEMENTAL CAUSAL SET

The fundamental causal element of all that happens. It is made up of an effect and its immediate causes that represents a single causal relationship. The causes consist of an action and one or more conditions. Causal Sets, like causes, can not exist alone. They are part of a continuum of causes with no beginning or end.

## EVENT

An interaction of several causes at a particular place and time.

## EVENT-BASED PROBLEMS

Problems that center around people, objects and rules that occur in time and space. Distinguished from rule-based problems by having more than one possible solution.

## EVIDENCE

Data used to conclude. Comes in different quality levels, Sensed by 5 senses, Inferred, Intuited, Emotionally Sensed.

## FACT

A cause supported by evidence.

## FAVORITE SOLUTION MINDSET

Our natural tendency to seek a familiar solution to problems based on some categorical assessment. An ineffective strategy most of the time.

## GARBAGE SOLUTION STRATEGY

Placing as many problems as possible into a category and then solving the problem categorically. Like the way we put all our garbage into a single container and it magically disappears. While the solution appears to work, it causes many other problems.

## GROOVENATION

The process of justifying our beliefs. It is physiological in origin and is found in our search to validate our existing realities.

## GROUPTHINK

The condition of relinquishing our individuality for the perceived common good of a group.

Apollonian Publications, LLC

## POINT OF IGNORANCE

When asking why, why, why, the point of ignorance is where we can honestly admit we don't know why. Only 1 in 20 people are capable of going there - most invent an answer and then stop.

## PRIMARY EFFECT

Any effect of consequence that we want to prevent from occurring.

## PROBLEM SOLVING

Overcoming a difficulty or undesired situation by implementing one or more solutions.

## PROTOTYPICAL TRUTHS

Conclusions about the world we live in that are subject to change given enough evidence to support a new conclusion. All our truths are prototypical, some are just more ensconced than others.

## ROOT CAUSE

Any cause in the cause continuum that is acted upon by a solution such that the problem does not recur. It is not the root cause we seek, it is effective solutions.

## RULE-BASED PROBLEMS

Problems that do not require people, objects, or time and space and always have a predefined right answer.

## SINGLE REALITY

Sometimes called the truth. Most humans believe there is a single reality that everyone can see, but what we fail to understand is that no two humans perceive the world the same. It is physiologically impossible for any two people to possess the same view of the world. With this dilemma, the best we can hope for is a common reality.

## SOLUTION KILLERS

Very judgmental statements used to kill a solution idea; e.g.: We already tried that once. Used by fearful people to resist change of any kind.

## STAKEHOLDER

A person or group with a stake in the success or failure of an enterprise or group.

### STORY TELLING
Communication describing an event by relating people, places, and things in a linear time frame from past to present.

### STRATEGY
An ordering process used by the mind to solve categorically recognized problems.

Apollonian Publications, LLC